Moving Power and Money

Moving Power and Money
The Politics of Census Taking

by Barbara Everitt Bryant
and William Dunn

New Strategist Publications, Inc.

Ithaca, New York

New Strategist Publications, Inc.
P.O. Box 242, Ithaca, New York 14851
607 / 273-0913

ISBN 0-9628092-7-6
Library of Congress Catalog Card Number 95-67315

Printed in the United States of America

To John, with whom I've pioneered new directions for a two-career family marriage for 46 years. And to Linda, Randy, and Lois, who grew up admirably despite having two working parents in an era when the other Moms stayed home. Finally, to my own Mother, Dad, and Uncle Ben, who lighted torches the rest of us have followed.

B.E.B.

For Betsy, Nora, Theresa, and Marie Murphy—the most loving and wonderful sister and nieces a guy could ever hope to have. With love and thanks.

W.D.

Table of Contents

Preface

The neighbors in Ann Arbor wondered when men in suits, driving unmarked cars, came knocking to inquire about my career, my character, and my personal habits. Did I use drugs? Drink excessively? Never, to anyone's knowledge—but then why hadn't the neighbors seen me around lately?

What seemed like needless snooping was part of a thorough FBI background check, which I expected and accepted. By now the rumor was widely (and I later learned intentionally) spread to anyone who read the Detroit newspapers or *The Washington Post*, that I was in line to be director of the Bureau of the Census, U.S. Department of Commerce, appointed by President George Bush.

Eventually the FBI determined that I—a senior vice-president of a Detroit market-research firm and a sixtysomething grandmother of five—never used a controlled substance or belonged to a subversive group. The General Counsel's Office of the Commerce Department informed the White House that my financial papers (and my husband's) were clean. And, while it wasn't asked of me back in 1989, I could have passed the nanny test that sank President Clinton's appointments, first of Zoë Baird and then of Kimba Wood, to the post of attorney general.

I passed muster and parachuted into the top census job on December 7, 1989—a day that both President Bush and I hoped would not live in infamy. I say "parachuted" because that's what it felt like. I had less than four months to cram for the biggest test of my life: to direct the $2.6 billion 1990 census, the fuel of intense controversy, numerous lawsuits, and continuous political strong-arming.

In the end, the 1990 census would count 249,632,692 people—922,819 of them overseas and 248,709,873 within the United States. The post-enumeration survey and demographic analysis—two follow-up checks on the accuracy of the count—showed that the census missed 1.6 percent (post-enumeration survey) to 1.8 percent (demographic analysis) of the population. This was the second lowest "undercount"—the Census Bureau's term for the people it misses—ever. As in previous censuses, the undercount rate was not the same for all segments of the population, however. It was as high as 5 percent among Hispanics and American Indians, 4 percent among Blacks, 4 percent among those living in rental housing, 2 percent among Asians and Pacific Islanders, 1 percent among non-Hispanic Whites, and almost zero among homeowners.

Coming from academic and private-sector research, where 70 to 90 percent response rates are cause for celebration, I consider the Census Bureau's record phenomenal. Neither the academic nor the private sector ever even attempts to survey one-quarter of a billion people. But this proved little comfort to mayors and assorted special-interest groups across the country who think the Census Bureau should count them all—even though they know they have many uncooperative constituents who regard the census as a bore, a chore, or an invasion of their privacy. Some say, "It's none of the government's damn business" how old they are, how much money they make, or how they get to work. They don't realize that this information is used by planners and businesses to provide the goods and services most of us want and need.

The Hot Seat

The job of Census Bureau director is an around-the-decade hot seat that warms up to electric-chair intensity every ten years at the time of the decennial census. The census is a feeding frenzy among governors, mayors, members of Congress, and even the general public. Each group wants the census to count as many people as possible in its jurisdiction.

The stakes are high and getting higher. More than a mere count of heads, the decennial census moves power. It determines the reapportionment of the entire House of Representatives and the redistricting of state legislatures and city and county councils across the country. It also moves money—billions of dollars in federal funds are distributed annually to states based on formulae that include census counts.

Census results also are a gold mine for researchers and businesses, from the basement entrepreneur to Pizza Hut and General Motors. In the hands of planners, developers, business managers, and investors, census statistics directly influence where they will locate apartments, homes, factories, schools, hospitals, malls, and offices. Ultimately, the census determines where jobs and money will—and won't—be.

Power, money, and sex are the three things that people fight about. The decennial census moves power and money. It also measures sex. That is, it counts both sexes.

Since the 1970s, when federal revenue sharing with states was initiated, cities sue the Census Bureau if they don't like their counts—and virtually none think their counts are large enough because people are money. And so, in this litigious age, they go to court. The 1980 census—the first to wind up in court despite being the most accurate census on record—became embroiled in 52 separate lawsuits. The 1990 census would trigger its first lawsuit, spearheaded by the City of New York, two years before

3

the actual counting began. With my appointment as director, my name moved onto the lawsuit as a defendant—the first of 20 suits in which I would become a defendant (a 21st was filed four years after the census, and after I left office).

Most of the lawsuits revolve around the persistent controversy over the undercount. What we know about the undercount comes from the bureau's own internal research into the problem. Intended as a design tool for improving the next census, this research helped cut the undercount from 5.4 percent in 1950 to a low of 1.2 percent in 1980. Unfortunately, that same research has been used effectively by plaintiffs as a weapon against the bureau.

"Never before have I been part of an organization that produces the whips with which it gets flogged. It's masochism," said John J. Connolly, my assistant director for communications at the Census Bureau.

Along with the growing concern about the differential undercount is Americans' growing concern about privacy. The two concerns—the one demanding that everyone stand up and be counted, and the other resisting the federal government's nosing about—are on a collision course. If a crash occurs, it will damage the 2000 census, limit how much we know about one another as a people, and hamper our economy in the 21st century.

Back Home in Ann Arbor

With the change in presidential administrations in 1993, I've returned from Washington, D.C., to Ann Arbor, where I am now a research scientist at the School of Business Administration at the University of Michigan.

Before I took the position of director of the Census Bureau, I decided to use whatever I learned during my tenure to improve the taking of the 2000 census. One of my main goals as director was to begin researching fundamental changes in census taking. Now as the former director, I am speaking, writing articles, and participating in panel discussions in favor of necessary changes in census taking that will not only protect the privacy of individuals, but also allow for the collection of the best possible statistics about our population and economy.

This book is a behind-the-scenes look at the role of the Census Bureau in the highly political, complex, and surprisingly dramatic census-taking process. The book also examines the players involved, not just at the Census Bureau, but on Capitol Hill, in city halls, the media, special-interest groups, and—most important of all—the American people.

In explaining the importance of taking a census every ten years, Census Bureau staffers are fond of paraphrasing a quote by Abraham Lincoln to the effect that "to know where you're going, you first have to know where you've been."

It is vital for our nation to be well informed about itself in order to choose the best course for the future. This book examines how privacy concerns, special interests, and a hostile public affected the 1990 census, and how they might affect future censuses. The impact of these concerns are important to each and every one of us and all of our communities.

Keep in mind that the next census will not only track the evolution of American society in the 1990s, but will provide the statistical portrait of America in the year 2000. This will set the nation's course for the first decade of the 21st century.

So, we had better get it right.

Barbara Everitt Bryant,
Director, Bureau of the Census, 1989-1993
Ann Arbor, Michigan

CHAPTER 1

The Census: Heartbeat of the Privacy Debate

In the United States, we are of two minds about information. As a nation, we are an open society, wanting and benefiting from the use of a lot of information. But as individuals, we get mighty squeamish about providing more than a minimal glimpse of ourselves. Most of us suffer from the name-rank-and-serial-number syndrome.

Ours is a country in which the slogan on the first official flag, raised by John Paul Jones in 1775, was: "Don't Tread on Me." Many Americans think this slogan means that "Big Brother" (i.e., the government) has no right to know about them. If Big Brother asks questions, Big Brother is invading their privacy.

In my role as Census Bureau director, and as the first woman director, I've occasionally been called Big Sister. I can assure you that I am not and never have been Big Sister. Nor is the Census Bureau Big Brother, although some persist in thinking so.

Despite our schizophrenia about revealing too much about ourselves, the vast majority of Americans—although not all—voluntarily respond to the census every ten years. As a nation we have been doing so since 1790 in what is now the longest-running periodic census in the world. It's the small proportion of people who don't respond who cause problems for the Census Bureau, and for their communities, mayors, governors, and Congressional representatives. Those who don't respond inflate the cost of census taking and distort census results. The number who didn't respond or were missed dropped from 1940 to 1980, but unfortunately rose in 1990.

Some people ignore the census out of indifference. Others avoid the census in a misguided effort to protect their privacy. A month before the 1990 census, a Gallup Poll reported that only 23 percent of Americans were "fully confident" that an individual's census results would be kept confidential, which is required by law. Another 44 percent were only "somewhat confident" that individual census data would be kept confidential. I'm certain that the confidence level of an ever more cynical public has not increased since then.

In the age of the information highway, many Americans feel that their privacy is increasingly under assault. Some believe the census is one of the assailants. The census, by design, is a tradeoff between the government's need to know for policy and planning purposes and the individual's right to total privacy. Though the census might invade people's privacy by asking questions, the results of the census benefit every community in the nation. On top of that, the Census Bureau guarantees each individual "confidentiality." Confidentiality means the promise, and the ability to keep the promise, that any questions you answer will remain confidential—not linked to your name for 72 years.

The Issues for 2000

The 2000 census is only a few years away. The first test of it took place in 1995. Based on my own experiences on the front lines of the 1990 census, I see two issues looming for 2000. Each is "priority number one" to a different constituency, and each is affected by an increasingly hostile public. The two priorities are:

COST. Congress is nearly apoplectic about the rising cost of the census. True, the cost has gone up much faster than inflation: from $8 per household in 1960 to $25 per household in 1990, all in 1990 dollars. The price tag for the 1990 census was $2.6 billion.

Still, that's only $1 per person per year—a bargain really. But Congress doesn't add things up that way. In the era of ballooning deficits and budget caps, legislators have the long knives out and aimed at the census budget. Yet growing public indifference and concerns about privacy mean more people are avoiding the census, making it costlier to find and count them.

UNDERCOUNT. "Costs be damned. Cut the differential undercount," is the top demand of governors, mayors, representatives, and advocates of the historically undercounted groups. Congressional representatives insist that solving the undercount problem is of near equal importance to cutting costs because of the effects of the undercount on the apportionment of Congress and because dissatisfied mayors complain to them first. It's likely, however, that the undercount will rise as our society grows more diverse and as more citizens resist government intrusion. The only ways to reduce the undercount are for the Census Bureau to access other government records of those who won't respond voluntarily, and to estimate statistically those who remain uncounted.

Some legislators believe one way to cut both cost and undercount is to reduce the number of questions asked by the census. This suggestion has alarmed many data users, who do not want to lose the wealth of information provided by the almost identical questions asked by the last three censuses. In fact, it's unlikely that shrinking the size of the census questionnaire would cut costs much or add significantly to response rates. Research shows that the marginal cost of each additional census question is small, and that nearly all of those who responded to the short census questionnaire (asked of all households) would have responded to the long questionnaire (asked of 17 percent of households). Privacy advocates are always on the side of "less is better" when it comes to asking people questions, however. One possible compromise: a shorter, more basic census coupled with large, ongoing sample surveys throughout the decade that would gather other necessary demographic and socioeconomic information.

The Testing Ground

The Census Bureau is trying to resolve these issues, looking for ways to count more people at lower cost. To do so, it fielded a test census in the spring of 1995 in three of the most difficult-to-count areas in the country: Oakland, California; northwestern Louisiana; and Paterson, New Jersey.

The Census Bureau also had planned to run the test in New Haven, Connecticut. But it had to cancel testing there because the final budget appropriation approved by Congress for 1995 was not enough to allow for four test sites. New Haven had been chosen as a test site because it is the home of Yale University. In analyzing why households did not return their 1990 census forms, bureau researchers found that in households where unrelated people live together, nobody takes responsibility for the household's paperwork.[1,2] This lowers the response to the census because census forms are mailed to addresses rather than individuals. When three or four students share an apartment, the census form may sit on the hall table for a while before somebody finally tosses it in the wastebasket. New Haven had been chosen as a test census site because it is home to many households of unrelated people and has a racially mixed population.

But the three sites that remained in the test offered plenty of challenges. Oakland, California, is one of the most diverse cities in the nation.[3] Unfortunately, experience has shown that diverse cities are hard to count for a variety of reasons including high rates of mobility, rental housing, new immigrants (legal and illegal), and pervasive mistrust of government. In the 1990 census, Oakland had an abysmally low response rate. Only half of

Oakland's residents voluntarily returned census questionnaires mailed to their households. Fortunately, the Census Bureau still makes house calls. It had to revert to the old-fashioned method of in-person interviews at non-responding households to complete the census.

One in five Oakland residents is foreign born; 12 percent arrived in the United States during the 1980s.[3] One-quarter speak a language other than English at home—either Spanish or an Asian language. The 1990 census reported that 44 percent of Oakland's residents are Black, 15 percent are Asian or Pacific Islander, and 14 percent are Hispanic. Language was clearly one of the important barriers to voluntary response in Oakland in 1990, since census questionnaires were available only in English and Spanish. Though the questionnaires came in only two languages, the Census Bureau's Oakland enumerators spoke 26 different languages. In New York, enumerators spoke 52 languages, making Oakland and New York City the most difficult cities in the country for census takers.

This is nothing new for New York. "The enumeration of the population of New York City has always been a matter of great difficulty and the results of the enumeration have often been questioned by city officials," then-director of the Census Bureau, W.M. Steuart, wrote in a 1923 letter that sounds like one I could have written. New York's leadership has cried "undercount" for at least 100 years. After the 1890 census, Mayor Hugh J. Grant had the police conduct a recount. The mayor failed to convince President Benjamin Harrison that the Census Bureau should do a recount because there were demonstrable errors in the police census.

In 1990 Rep. Charles E. Schumer of Queens, a self-appointed spokesperson for New York City on behalf of its pro-adjustment lawsuit, complained to the media, "I think the Census Bureau really believes they are still counting people as if they lived in Salina, Kansas, in 1890." [4]

Schumer is a colorful Democratic congressman and master of the 15-second sound bite. The media love him because he is always good for a caustic, witty quip on whatever issue is riding high at the moment. I found Schumer far more fun to watch in 1994 as he spearheaded legislation for banning assault weapons than I did when his quips portrayed the 1990 census team as naive incompetents trying to count big-city people just like we count those in small cities. In fact, the Census Bureau doesn't count New Yorkers the same way at all because the people of Salina, Kansas, are far more cooperative than those in New York and other big cities. Salina, Kansas, doesn't have high concentrations of public housing where the Census Bureau has to send enumerators in teams for their own safety, and it doesn't have residents who speak a United Nations array of languages.

In 1990, 63 percent of households in the state of Kansas voluntarily returned their census forms. This was much higher than the rate in New York City, which ranged from only 40 percent in central Brooklyn to 57 percent in southwest Queens and the northwest Bronx. But Kansas' 63 percent in 1990 was much worse than its 78 percent return rate of 1980. Non-response is a growing problem, even in middle America.

"Don't you dare close out census counting in New York City or Oakland before Salina, Kansas!" C. Louis Kincannon, deputy director of the Census Bureau, told field operations. That and one of Kincannon's other homilies will be remembered in planning census 2000. His other homily: "Never rent a census district office under an abortion clinic." One district office was saved by a midnight phone call informing the local manager that water was pouring from the office on the floor above, where anti-abortion activists had attacked an abortion clinic with water hoses.

Although we had to make some house calls in Salina, too, there was no danger of finishing there after New York or Oakland. With their variety of people and housing, house calls in New York City and Oakland took far longer than those in Salina. That's why the bureau picked Oakland as one of three test sites for the 2000 census. If the Census Bureau can find a way to boost the count and lower costs in Oakland, then what it learns may be transferable to other hard-to-count areas. But New York City will remain a unique case in every census.

There are virtually no immigrants in the six rural, hilly parishes of northwestern Louisiana, which was the second site for the 1995 test census. The parishes of Bienville, De Soto, Jackson, Natchitoches, Red River, and Winn represent stability: 85 percent of their residents were born in Louisiana. Nationally, only 67 percent of Americans live in the state in which they were born. The parishes of northwestern Louisiana are different than the nation in other ways as well. With a population that is 40 percent Black and 60 percent non-Hispanic White, the parishes have virtually none of the other ethnic or racial segments that comprise the U.S. population. Education levels are lower than those of the rest of the United States—only 58 to 64 percent of adults (levels vary by parish) are high-school graduates compared to the national average of 75 percent; only 9 to 16 percent are college graduates compared to a national rate of 20 percent. The poverty level is substantially higher in the six parishes than in the nation as a whole—24 to 35 percent poor compared to the U.S.'s 13 percent.

In this part of northwestern Louisiana, where the pace is slow and the backwoods roads meander, over one-fifth of housing units are mobile homes. The people living in those mobile homes at the time of the last census may have been born in Louisiana, or even in the same parish, but do their homes sit on the same cement blocks in 1995 as they did when they were geographically coded in 1990? Or are they—as their name implies—truly "mobile"? To answer that question, the bureau used sophisticated technology in the 1995 test that it developed for the 1990 census—the Topologically Integrated Geographic Encoding and Referencing System, otherwise known as the TIGER system. TIGER is a computerized mapping system of all 7 million "blocks" in the nation.

While most of us think of "blocks" as something we walk around in cities, Census Bureau geographers divide rural areas into blocks as well. The difference is that out in the country a block might be a mile long and one-half mile wide, with rural roads or state highways as boundaries. In the census, every resident of the United States is identified by the block on which he or she usually lives, or the block where he or she was counted (e.g., if the person lives in a shelter or on the street). The TIGER database contains the latitude and longitude points along every street, road, or highway that bounds the nation's 7 million blocks. Only about 3 million of those blocks contain occupied housing units.

For the test census, the Census Bureau merged its TIGER maps with a computer list of addresses from the 1990 census, creating for the first time a permanent master address file. The bureau will continuously update this permanent file with the help of the U.S. Postal Service, which will alert the bureau to new addresses and streets. Never before has the bureau had a permanent address file. Instead, it has constructed address files from scratch with each new census—a complex and costly procedure.

Like the names of individuals, the bureau's address lists have been strictly confidential in the past, despite pressure by localities to make the information public. This made adversaries of local communities and the Census Bureau. Communities did not trust the completeness of census address lists. The bureau did not trust communities to refrain from using census lists for activities such as zoning enforcement—in census taking, the bureau invariably finds some illegal housing units. Such enforcement would breach the guarantee of confidentiality the bureau makes to all it counts.

A compromise has been reached for the future, reflected in the Census Address List Improvement Act of 1994. This Act was proposed to Congress by the bureau. It amends the law that makes census records confidential, allowing the bureau to use local government and post office information to improve the master address file for 2000 and beyond. Local officials, designated as "census liaisons," will be given copies of the address lists for their jurisdictions so that they can verify their completeness and accuracy. The liaisons must maintain the confidentiality of the lists and are prohibited from using them for local purposes. Procedures for adjudicating disputes are being developed so that local governments and the Census Bureau can agree on the lists before the census takes place—a big improvement over crying "foul" and going to court as in the last two censuses.

There is nothing easy about the areas in which the Census Bureau chose to field the 1995 test census. The third test site, Paterson, New Jersey, has changed a lot in the past generation, from a White, blue-collar, working-class community to one that is 41 percent Hispanic and 36 percent Black. Two-thirds of its housing units are rentals. In half of them the people speak a language other than English. While the 1990 undercount was only 1.6 to 1.8 percent overall nationally, among renters it was 4.3 percent.

Balancing Conflicting Goals

As the Census Bureau attempts to raise response rates to the census, it is caught between society's need for information and the public's resistance to revelation. The politicians don't make the job any easier.

"The 1990 census was far too costly and inaccurate, and the results were delayed considerably," noted the House Appropriations Committee, which holds the purse strings for the Census Bureau, in a message on the 1994 budget. "These problems will only increase unless there are significant changes in the approach in taking the decennial census."

The Census Bureau agrees that there is need for change, which is why the bureau began to research new methods of census taking in 1991. But Congress doesn't do the bureau any favors, because the politicians want more for less. The House Appropriations Committee cut the bureau's $23 million request for census 2000 research and development to just $8 million in 1994. They were more generous in 1995, recognizing the importance of research and testing. But the final appropriation for 1995 was only enough to test the census at three sites, rather than the four originally planned.

The Census Bureau has learned that throwing more enumerators (and consequently more money) at those who can't or won't answer the census cannot reduce the undercount further. The bureau hit the wall in 1990. It greatly expanded its efforts to reach undercounted groups. Nevertheless, the results fell short of those in 1980—a net undercount of 1.6 to 1.8 percent in 1990, up from a net 1.2 percent undercount in 1980 (I use the term "net" because some undercount is offset by overcount, or people who are counted twice).

So the bureau is looking for other ways to boost response. It has redesigned the census questionnaire, for example. It was too late to change the design of the census questionnaire by the time I became director because questionnaires were already rolling off the presses. The mail-out package dismayed me with its complexity. After people opened the envelope, they were forced to unravel a questionnaire folded up like an AAA road map. Then out fell an instruction folder, a flyer with motivational messages explaining why the census was important to answer, and a return envelope.

The result was a flurry of paper, the kind you automatically put in the "to do later" pile. All this was for a questionnaire that, for 83 percent of households, asked only seven questions about each person in the household and seven more about the housing unit itself. Coming from private-sector survey research where we try to make questionnaires look easy to answer, I couldn't imagine why the Census Bureau had come up with a design that made an easy questionnaire look difficult.

Then there was the layout and typography. It was designed to be machine-friendly (i.e., readable by scanners), but ended up being people-hostile. The questionnaire was even harder to fathom for the 17 percent who got the long-form version with an additional 19 housing unit and 26 individual questions. As Deputy Director Kincannon said, reporting back to me from a trip to Texas, "You can't imagine how a census long form breaks up the week in El Paso."

"When is the second mailing scheduled?" I asked during my early briefings at the Census Bureau. Academic and private-sector surveyors know from experience that they can increase the response to a mail survey significantly by sending a second mailing to non-respondents.

"There isn't time for one," I was informed. "We don't think it would be as cost-effective as starting follow-up with household calls immediately." My jaw dropped.

Soon after that, I brought to the bureau a nationally recognized academic, survey methodologist Robert M. Groves, from the Survey Research Center of the University of Michigan. He recruited another well-known researcher, Donald A. Dillman from Washington State University, to start work on census 2000. They designed tests that proved the merits of advance and reminder mailings and of sending replacement questionnaires to non-responding households. The cost of extra mailings is more than offset by the savings in follow-up calls. Dillman also designed the people-friendly questionnaires used in the 1995 test census. Not only are they much easier to read, they are also easier to pass around among a group of unrelated people who share an apartment so that each can fill out his or her own section.

Of the $2.6 billion spent on the 1990 census, the bureau spent somewhere between $490 million and $560 million following up on those who did not respond to the mailed questionnaires, or roughly 20 percent of the total census budget.[5] A big change planned for the 2000 census, and one likely to cause the greatest furor over privacy, is the use of sampling and estimation to lower costs and improve the count. By not trying to chase down every missing household, the Census Bureau can devote more resources to pursuing a sample of households far more intensively at lower cost.

Estimates produced from an intensively contacted sample should be more accurate than additional numbers emerging after months of hunting for everyone. No nation in the world spends as much time taking its census as the United States. Yet the more time that passes after census day, the less accurate people's memories are about where they were on April 1. And even with the effort to track down 100 percent of the missing, an appreciable proportion remain unreached. Of those who did not respond by mail in 1990, 20 percent of those in central cities, 12 percent of those in the suburbs, and 11 percent of those in rural areas were counted only by enumerators who asked their neighbors, landlords, or postal carriers about them.

Even if the Census Bureau follows up on a sample of households rather than all of the missing, some of the sampled households will remain uninterviewed. This raises the issue of how else to account for the missing. It also raises the issue of privacy. One way to find the missing is to tap into other government data, such as Aid to Families with Dependent Children records, public housing files, school enrollment figures, local tax records, and so on. As a last resort, should the Census Bureau access these records? It has the right to do so.

According to Section 6 of the census law, known as Title 13, the secretary of commerce may (a) call upon any other department, agency, or establishment of the federal government or the government of the District of Columbia, for information; (b) purchase reports and records from states, counties, cities, or other units of government; and (c) acquire information from any other source instead of conducting direct inquiries. Once individual data from other sources are added to the census, they come under the confidentiality protection of Title 13.

For the population censuses, the Census Bureau has rarely used its power to access other records—other than to purchase commercial mailing lists for building its address file—largely to avoid raising concerns about privacy. For the economic censuses and surveys, the bureau uses IRS business tax filings from very small businesses to save those businesses from the burden of filling out census forms.

For the 1990 census, the bureau obtained state records of the names and addresses of parolees and probationers. Bureau research had showed that many in this group were missed by the 1980 census. The bureau matched the names from state records against the names on census forms filled out at the official home addresses of parolees and probationers. It turned out that about one-third of parolees and probationers had not been included on these census forms. After the bureau added their names to the census, it would be 72 years before anyone could see them. To improve the census count in 2000, the bureau is considering using more non-census records like these.

Americans' schizophrenia about the uses of information puts census 2000 between a rock and a hard place. The rock is the political necessity to count as many people as possible. The hard place is the resistance of some of the public to being counted. These two opposing forces make it certain that someone will sue the Census Bureau long before 2000. The first lawsuit of the 1980 census was filed by Detroit on Census Day 1980, just as the count was getting under way. The first lawsuit of the 1990 census was filed by New York City in 1988, two years before the census took place. Some special-interest group is likely to jump-start census 2000 with a suit in 1995 or 1996.

The suit could come from an advocacy group intent on protecting the privacy of a particular constituency—an undercounted group that politicians want fully counted. More likely, the first suit will come from those who think that estimating the missing rather than actually tracking them down will enlarge someone else's pie at the expense of their own. The Census Bureau won all of the 52 suits filed against it regarding the 1980 census, the last settled in 1987. Most of the lawsuits regarding the 1990 census had been settled by mid-decade in the Census Bureau's favor, but the New York City suit (discussed in Chapters 3 and 9) keeps unfolding and several other suits are pending.

No matter who throws the first stone, the census and the Census Bureau stand at a crossroads. Will Americans come to accept the need for the most accurate information about themselves to make rational decisions in the 21st century? Or will our trust and faith in one another, as embodied by the census, continue to erode? As Americans close the blinds, they send our country stumbling into the future.

References

1. Fay, Robert, Nancy Bates and Jeffrey Moore (1991). "Lower Mail Response in the 1990 Census: A Preliminary Interpretation," *Proceedings, 1991 Annual Research Conference,* (Washington, D.C.: Bureau of the Census), p. 26.

2. Kulka, Richard A., Nicholas Holt, Woody Carter, and Kathryn L. Dowd (1991). "Self-Reports of Time Pressure, Concerns for Privacy, and Participation in the 1990 Mail Census," *Proceedings, 1991 Annual Research Conference* (Washington, D.C.: Bureau of the Census), pp. 44, 49.

3. Bureau of the Census. The data on the demographic characteristics of the test sites come from the 1990 census, STF1A and STF3A.

4. Sirica, Jack (1990). "Census Counts on Promotional Blitz," *Newsday,* January 14, 1990, p. 7.

5. Panel to Evaluate Alternative Census Methods, Committee on National Statistics, Commission on Behavioral and Social Sciences and Education, National Research Council (1994). *Counting People in the Information Age,* (Washington, D.C.: National Academy Press, 1994), p. 98.

CHAPTER 2

Privacy Rights Versus Public Good

Health-care reform in the late 1990s—maybe. A health security card for each resident of the U.S.—not so fast!

As policy makers tried to hammer out a health-care package in the mid-1990s, and hammered at each other, one controversial proposal that alarmed privacy advocates was President Clinton's call for an individual health insurance card. This card would include an encoded computer chip that would give doctors or hospitals access to a central data bank with the cardholder's medical records. To many, the proposal summoned up the specter of an intrusive government that knows too much. Critics of health security cards warn of snoopers who would dig through government databases to look up people's medical records for nefarious reasons.

The fear is not groundless. During the 1992 presidential campaign, Bill Clinton's own passport file was improperly searched by at least one member of the Bush administration's State Department who was fishing for possible campaign ammunition. And after Clinton's election, some of his aides made questionable forays into files of former Bush staffers.

The fear of Big Brother has become a part of the immigration debate as well. The American Civil Liberties Union, as well as Hispanic, Chinese, and Jewish groups, raised alarms about job discrimination when the federal Advisory Commission on Immigration Reform proposed that the government establish a computerized registry of the names and Social Security numbers of all citizens and aliens authorized to work in the United States.[1]

These incidents are but pieces of the larger, troubling issue: how do we protect personal privacy in the computer age, when information has become an invaluable resource?

The Census Bureau is central to this issue, not just because the bureau asks questions many people consider personal. It's also because of proposals under serious consideration to allow the Census Bureau to use its authority to dip into other government records to gather population information. And it's because census 2000 will use a computerized master address file (addresses without names) to locate us. While most other countries—including democratic nations—have long had population registers and/or national address registers to facilitate the planning and taking of censuses (in a few countries these have actually replaced censuses), the United States does not have such a registry, in large part because of privacy concerns. This surprises many who assume the Postal Service has one big, all-inclusive list. It does not.

As a result, two or more years before every census, the Census Bureau has assembled an address list from scratch. It pulls the addresses together from commercial mailing lists and from visual inspection of addresses by census workers, including rural households that receive their mail at post office boxes. For the last several censuses, the Census Bureau has then contracted with the U.S. Postal Service to check the addresses for deliverability. Despite all this legwork, several million census forms mailed by the bureau were returned by the post office as non-deliverable in 1990.

This address-building process is not only laborious, but also costly, time consuming, and prone to error. The errors, in turn, trigger lawsuits by mayors and special-interest groups who want access to the lists to correct errors and boost their populations.

In the past, the bureau has repeatedly fought those who try to gain access to its lists, asserting that the lists, as well as individual census information, are confidential and cannot be released under census law. That has changed since passage of the Census Address List Improvement Act of 1994, which allows sharing with local governments and the Postal Service. However, local governments are prohibited from making any use of the lists beyond improving census-taking accuracy.

Creating a permanent master address file, checked and updated by local governments (who don't trust the accuracy of the Census Bureau lists now) could cut down on lawsuits. Maybe. But the use of the master address file could raise the hackles of civil libertarians who object on privacy grounds.

Testifying before Congress, Laura Murphy Lee of the American Civil Liberties Union recommended address sharing only as a one-way, not a two-way exchange. "The Census Bureau may obtain address lists provided that it maintains confidentiality of information. Too great a risk to privacy is posed by sharing information with other agencies and state and local governments, including USPS. If the USPS is to share this information, it must be required to uphold conditions of confidentiality." [2]

USPS has a law of its own, Title 39, which prohibits the sharing of its own data. The 1994 law was necessary before USPS and the bureau could exchange with each other.

Ironically, our country's lack of a population registry or address list, plus the Census Bureau's policy of releasing data only in the aggregate rather than at the individual level, have spawned an industry of information vendors who are in turn adding fuel to the privacy debate.

Credit card companies, department stores, magazines, mail-order catalogs, banks, and other businesses collect revealing socioeconomic data about their customers as a by-product of doing business. Many businesses sell their customer information to list brokers who compile it into databases that categorize consumers by demographics, psychographics, and lifestyles. These databases are repackaged into segmented mailing lists bought by other businesses hoping to gain new customers.

Linking Databases: Threat to Privacy?

Computer technology makes it relatively simple to link the individual information reported on an application for a mortgage or a warranty card with other data, such as magazine subscriptions, credit card charges, and automobile or voter registration lists. Unknown to many people, automobile owner lists are sold by 34 of the 50 states, and many states sell lists of registered voters.

Americans voluntarily submit their names and other vital statistics to those who request them because they want a mortgage, a magazine, or a credit card. Nevertheless, in the public's view, some of the private database builders have gone too far. Lotus and Equifax had to scuttle plans to sell a huge database of consumer names that was to be called Lotus Marketplace. This product was scheduled to go on the market in the early 1990s. It would have included the addresses, shopping habits, and other characteristics of 120 million households, according to advertising claims. (Somehow, Lotus managed to come up with 18 million more households than the 102 million the Census Bureau counted in the U.S. at that time.)

Selling such a comprehensive list of names and addresses linked to shopping habits had never before been attempted. And it didn't get the reception Lotus was hoping for. While marketers were eager to get their hands on the product, many special-interest groups, private citizens, and legislators denounced it as yet another threat to privacy.

Public opposition was so great that Lotus and Equifax had

to withdraw the product. Although the two companies insist that they were sensitive to privacy concerns, their early promotional efforts implied that the database contained census data. This suggestion confused many and threatened the public's perception of the Census Bureau's integrity.

Business databases that claim to include census data do not—and by law cannot—include individual census records. Instead, they link names and addresses compiled from mailing lists to the characteristics of the census block group (or approximately 300 to 400 households, the smallest geographic level for which the Census Bureau releases detailed characteristics) or census tract (approximately 1,000 households) in which those addresses are located. This information may show that someone lives in a neighborhood with a median income of $45,000; with mostly owner-occupied, single-family homes; and in which 20 percent of residents have graduated from college.

If you live in this census tract, you may not share these characteristics, however. You might be a single man, renting an apartment in one of the few apartment complexes located in the tract. You might have a post-graduate degree and earn $125,000 a year. By law, your name and address cannot be linked to your specific characteristics as collected by the census. If your name and address turn up in a database linked to your income or other characteristics, then you submitted the information yourself— perhaps on an application for a bank loan, for example. So, when the dinner-time call comes from an annoying telemarketer, blame yourself—not the Census Bureau.

While the Census Bureau is by far the largest collector of statistics for the federal government, it is no Big Brother. The bureau follows strict confidentiality laws. Unfortunately not all databases are so well guarded.

Count Me Out

Research clearly shows rising public alarm over threats to privacy and confidentiality. These fears adversely affect people's perceptions of the Census Bureau.

The 1990 census itself quantified mounting resistance and wariness. Those in only 63 percent of housing units voluntarily returned questionnaires promptly, requiring costly follow-up visits, down from 75 percent in 1980, and 78 percent in 1970. With a 12 percentage point drop in the voluntary response rate between 1980 and 1990, how low will it go in 2000? In all three censuses, about 10 percent of non-responding housing units proved to be vacant.

"When the public attitude is not good, the census suffers," said my predecessor, John G. Keane. The public attitude is not good. A 1993 Louis Harris and Associates poll found that a record 83 percent of Americans were concerned about intrusions into their privacy, up from 34 percent in 1970. Fifty-three percent were "very concerned" about their privacy, double the proportion just 15 years earlier.

Why this growing concern? According to Alan F. Westin, editor and publisher of the bimonthly newsletter, *Privacy & American Business,* "Growing privacy worries are due to a general distrust of institutions and the government process, and to public fears about the misuse of computer technology." [3]

So serious is the problem, and so far-reaching are the potential repercussions, that the highly respected National Academy of Sciences (including its Committee on National Statistics, its Commission on Behavioral and Social Sciences and Education, and its National Research Council) and the Social Science Research Council convened a panel to study the impact of privacy concerns. The 274-page report of the Panel on Confidentiality and Data Access, entitled *Private Lives and Public Policies,* asserts, "Many citizens believe increasingly and with some justification that their privacy is being eroded by organizations that develop and control the use of large databases that contain detailed information about them. They see the linkage of data from different sources as a particular threat. For these and other reasons, statistical agencies are finding it more difficult to persuade persons and organizations to participate in statistical surveys, whether voluntary or mandatory." [4]

The Panel on Confidentiality and Data Access is the latest of a growing list of organizations to investigate the subject. Others include the Privacy Protection Study Commission (1977), the American Statistical Association's Ad Hoc Committee on Privacy and Confidentiality (1977), the Conference on Computers, Freedom, and Privacy (1991, 1992), the Economic Policy Council Working Group, not to mention the American Civil Liberties Union's Privacy and Technology Project, as well as the Census Bureau's own Census Advisory Committees.

As confidence and trust in government institutions have declined over the past few decades, Americans' anxiety over privacy—or the lack of it—has steadily grown. People are more worried today, according to survey data, than they were in the wake of Watergate in the early 1970s, or following the savings-and-loan scandal of the 1980s.

The problem is especially acute among many of America's newer immigrants, particularly those who fled civil war or state oppression in their native countries. Experience has made them fearful of the knock at the door and distrustful of any government. New immigrants often do not understand or believe the Census Bureau's promise of confidentiality. Such rights did not exist in their homelands. Additionally, many immigrants don't speak English. Almost 10 million people are expected to immigrate to the U.S. in the 1990s—more people to add to the many millions of Americans already worried about protecting what's left of their privacy.

This sense of unease directly contributes to the undercount problem. Those who are most concerned about their privacy—undocumented immigrants, those who think their income is nobody's business but their own, families doubled up in violation of leases, landlords cramming renters into illegal basement apartments, and the floating homeless population, as well as legal immigrants fearful of any government questions—respond to such palpable fears by not answering the census. As these and other privacy worries rise, so will the undercount.

Changing Census Rules on Confidentiality

Americans' concerns about privacy are as old as the census, which is almost as old as the republic. The confidentiality of census results is now protected by law, but this wasn't always the case.

The Constitution, which requires a census every ten years for reapportionment of Congress, says nothing about privacy. It was Amendment IV, one of the first ten amendments ratified on December 15, 1791, that took the first stab at asserting a general right of privacy. It reads: "The right of the people to be secure in their persons, houses, papers, and effects, against unreasonable searches and seizures, shall not be violated, and no Warrants shall issue, but upon probable cause, supported by Oath or affirmation, and particularly describing the place to be searched, and the persons or things to be seized."

The first census, directed by Thomas Jefferson in 1790, took 18 months to complete and counted 3,929,326 people in 13 states and three territories. Reaction to the monumental effort was a foreshadowing of things to come two centuries down a road that would become the information highway. James Madison labeled the census of 1790 "a waste of trouble and supply materials for idle people to make a book."[5] Sound familiar?

President George Washington complained of an undercount caused by an uncooperative and fearful citizenry. He laid the blame on layabouts, religious zealots, tax opponents, and people with something to hide. Like mayors, governors, and presidents throughout American history, Washington wanted and expected a higher count because of the political clout it would bring.

In a letter to census director Jefferson, Washington fumed: "This you are to take along with it, that the real number will greatly exceed the official return, because, from religious scruples, some would not give in their lists; from an apprehension that it was intended as the foundation of a tax, others concealed or diminished theirs; and from the indolence of the mass and want of activity in many of the deputy enumerators, numbers are omitted." [6]

Prior to the census of 1850, census results were posted in each municipality and population center, listing the names of families, as a way of identifying who hadn't been counted. Census enumerators were not required to take an oath of non-disclosure until 1890. At that time, the concern was about revealing sensitive information about property or business, not personal characteristics, according to census historians Frederick G. Bohme and David M. Pemberton, in "Privacy and Confidentiality in the U.S. Censuses—A History." [7]

The first presidential proclamation regarding census confidentiality came in 1910. President William Howard Taft asserted: "There need be no fear that any disclosure will be made regarding any individual person or his affairs...Every employee of the Census Bureau is prohibited, under heavy penalty, from disclosing any information that may thus come to his knowledge." [8]

Despite the promise, Bohme and Pemberton report that "census confidentiality left something to be desired in 1910. There were numerous cases of over- and undercounting that had to be investigated and resolved." [9] Evidence clearly indicated that unauthorized, unsworn people helped gather household information in some cities—a clear breach of confidentiality.

Then, as now, those attempting to get a look at census files were trying to boost their census counts and protect their political turf. In the reapportionments that followed the first 13 censuses from 1790 to 1910, the government added Congressional seats to keep pace with a quickly-growing nation. The number of seats in the House of Representatives went from 106 in 1790 to 435 in 1910. [10]

Then, in 1911, a majority of Congress voted to fix the number of seats at 435. Each state got at least one seat. After that, seats were allocated according to population. Ever since, reapportionment has been a zero-sum game of winners and losers. Fast-growing states gain seats at the expense of slow-growing or declining ones.

This boosted the stakes tremendously. It made the census, always contentious, now a controversy. The first census to be conducted under the new rules of reapportionment—the 1920 census—was arguably the most controversial ever. The results were so surprising, significant, and disputed that Congress argued about them for over a decade. So bitter was the debate that Congress failed (actually, it refused) to reapportion the 435 seats of the House of Representatives. This was the only time in our history that this has happened.

The census data revealed that between 1910 and 1920 the United States had shifted from a rural to an urban nation. In 1910, a majority of the population lived in rural areas. By 1920, a majority lived in cities and towns. This was a shift that the rural-dominated Congress did not believe. Senators and Congressmen, threatened with diminished political power, were outraged. They claimed—what else—an undercount of rural residents. Not only did they fear a loss of power, but the rural representatives saw power slipping away to cities dominated by newly arrived immigrants.

Congress should have completed reapportionment based on the 1920 census by 1922. But it fought over the results until 1929. At that point, so close to the 1930 census, reapportionment was put on hold to await the 1930 results. So, for 20 years, from 1912 to 1932, rural America clung to a numerical advantage in Congressional seats, before losing it to urban America as a result of the 1930 census.

The first major challenge to the evolving concept and practice of census confidentiality came during World War I. The Census Bureau, in response to requests for information about men's ages, provided this information to the Justice Department and local draft boards.

While census takers and other officials in the bureau were sworn under oath, and under penalty of fine and prosecution, to keep information on individuals and businesses confidential, the director was given more leeway in extreme cases. World War I was judged to be an extreme case. In 1917, the Solicitor General held that the "Director of the Census might in the exercise of his discretion, furnish to the officials in charge of the execution of the Selective Service Law, information in regard to the names and ages of individuals, as it did not appear that any person would be harmed by the furnishing of such information for the purpose for which it was desired." [11]

Following World War I, the director of the Census Bureau gave the Department of Justice census information on the citizenship of people in Toledo in connection with deportation cases. In 1921 the bureau compiled names and addresses of people who were illiterate and sent the list to several states that were mounting literacy programs. In all of these cases, the release of confidential information was authorized at the discretion of the director.

Census Bureau historians Bohme and Pemberton caution in their study of census confidentiality, "These were all legitimate census uses in their times, and should not be cited as reasons for noncompliance with the censuses today." [12]

The Census Bureau's director did not comply with a 1930 request, however. This was from a federal agency called the Women's Bureau. It wanted the names, addresses, and employment status of women in Rochester, New York. While the mission of the Women's Bureau was to improve living and working conditions for women, Bohme and Pemberton note: "Perhaps given a heightened concern about confidentiality, the Census Bureau referred the request to the attorney general, who decided such information could not be released." [13]

Clearly, during the early decades of the 20th century, the bureau's confidentiality policy was too loose, susceptible to varying interpretation. Creating a coherent and tough confidentiality policy was hobbled by the fact that the rules changed every ten years, when Congress was required to pass authorizing legislation to take the next census. In so doing, it also wrote the regulations on how to conduct the count. These regulations lurched in different directions decade by decade.

Attempts to gain access to confidential census data during World War II ignited a controversy that still lives today. It eventually focused Congressional and public attention on the need to formulate and enforce an intelligent, consistent, and strict standard of confidentiality.

After the Japanese attack on Pearl Harbor and America's entry into the war, the War Department requested the names and addresses of all Japanese and Japanese-Americans enumerated in the 1940 census in the Western states.

The Census Bureau rejected the request. But the bureau did give the War Department punch cards, without names or addresses, identifying census tracts and other small areas with high concentrations of Japanese. "The military authorities thus knew where to concentrate their efforts to intern these people," write Bohme and Pemberton. "But in no case did the Census Bureau, contrary to law, furnish information about individuals that could be used to their detriment."[14] Additionally, bureau defenders contend that the population counts provided to the military were already available in published reports. Even today, the Census Bureau promises confidentiality only to individuals. Neighborhood characteristics, including their racial and ethnic mix, are available to all and much in demand by racial and ethnic groups.

The Japanese-Americans who lost property and were interned simply because of their ancestry see things differently, indeed. Their devastating fate has been cited repeatedly by critics as a breach in spirit, if not in fact, of census confidentiality. Critics say this is clear proof of the tenuous nature of any promise of confidentiality.

In the late 1940s, another agency attempted to gain access to confidential census documents. The Federal Bureau of Investigation sought unsuccessfully to get census data about people living in the neighborhood surrounding Blair House, where President Harry Truman lived while the White House was being restored. This time, the Census Bureau resisted the intrusion into its files.

Clearly, something needed to be done to clarify the boundaries. In 1954, Congress totally overhauled census confidentiality regulations by writing a single, permanent law that is clear, concise, complete, and has teeth. It is Title 13 of the U.S. Code. Not only does Title 13 require census information to be used only for statistical purposes, but it prohibits publication of the data in which any individual business or person can be identified. Thus, it limits release of census information to the aggregate level. The law makes answering the census mandatory (subject to a $100 fine). It also states that no one other than sworn officers and employees of the Census Bureau and its parent Department of Commerce is allowed to examine individual survey and census reports. All sworn officers and employees, including temporary employees, take a non-disclosure oath of confidentiality. [15]

The penalties for breaching confidentiality are stiff: up to a $5,000 fine and/or up to five years' imprisonment. These penalties apply to former as well as present employees. Census data on individuals or establishments are not subject to disclosure under the Freedom of Information Act. However, Title 13 does allow each person access to his or her own census information upon written request and payment of a fee. In addition, copies of the census questionnaire kept by the individual who supplied the data "shall be immune from legal process, and shall not, without the consent of the individual or establishment concerned, be admitted as evidence or used for any purpose in any action, suit, or other judicial or administrative proceeding."

As a safeguard, the Census Bureau separates names and addresses on completed census forms from the computer files containing the answers to census questions. In an activity known as disclosure avoidance, the bureau also masks even aggregate data if the numbers might identify a particular person or business. [16] For example, if you are the only household earning $1 million in your block group of 300 to 400 households, your income data will be swapped with that of someone otherwise similar to you in another nearby block group where there are more people with such salaries. In this way, income data for the larger area (probably a census tract) are accurate, but no one can snoop around your neighborhood to figure out who the millionaire is.

Individual census data are parked well off of the information highway. The computers containing individual census data are not a part of any computer network outside the bureau. Access to confidential information housed in the Census Bureau's computers is blocked by special, secure, dedicated data transmission lines. The staff changes coded passwords frequently to prevent unauthorized entry into the bureau's computers.

No one, no matter how high the authority, can obtain individual data from the Census Bureau. The airtight law covers the president, the White House, the Supreme Court, the military, the Internal Revenue Service, the Immigration Service, welfare agencies—everyone.

The confidentiality of individual census data lasts for 72 years. After that, anyone is allowed access to microfilm of individual returns through the National Archives, under Title 44 of the U.S. Code enacted in 1952. This access assists historians and other professional researchers. It provides a treasure trove to genealogists, as well as those interested in searching their own family roots. The most recent census data available from the archives are the forms from the controversial 1920 census, which ignited the rural/urban battle in Congress.

"The controversies sort of go away after 72 years," remarked Charlie Jones, the Census Bureau executive in charge of the 1990 census, in March of 1992. We both were still licking our wounds from 1990. Along with Don Wilson, director of the National Archives, I was about to cut the ribbon to give 300 eager people—mostly genealogists and family history buffs—lined up in a fifth floor corridor of the archives access to microfilms of the 1920 forms. None of those in line mentioned, or appeared to know or care about, the rural/urban controversy and failure to reapportion following the 1920 census.

Privacy Law: Limited in Scope

While Title 13 spells out the Census Bureau's confidentiality policy and Title 44 imposes the 72-year limit on confidentiality, these strict regulations actually say nothing about privacy.

It was only in the wake of Watergate and the resulting mistrust of government that Congress enacted the Privacy Act of 1974. This law covers federal government information about individuals, but it is clearly from a different decade and surprisingly limited in scope. It applies only to data on identifiable individuals—data that could be linked to someone's name. Briefly, it requires that federal agencies grant individuals access to their identifiable records (for example, census forms or IRS tax forms); ensure that existing information is accurate and timely; limit the collection of unnecessary information; and limit the disclosure of identifiable information to third parties. [17]

The Act details the circumstances when access to government files is permissible for legitimate or routine uses. But it says absolutely nothing about the gathering or dissemination of non-government records, such as credit card purchases. The Act also says nothing about surveillance and other forms of snooping, whether high-tech eavesdropping or low-tech keyhole spying.

The *Private Lives and Public Policies* report of the National Research Council and the Social Science Research Council points out that, "In contrast to the lax protection of statistical records under the Privacy Act of 1974, the statutory protection of statistical information collected by the Census Bureau under Title 13 of the U.S. Code is extremely rigorous." [18] And even an executive of the American Civil Liberties Union, which considers itself the guardian of individual liberties, says that "the Census Bureau has a history and track record of maintaining the confidentiality of census data." [19]

The councils warn: "Many agencies not covered by specific confidentiality legislation have to rely on the Privacy Act to protect identifiable data on individuals. There are serious limitations to the protections provided by the Privacy Act for data from individuals, however."

One limitation of the Privacy Act is that it does not prohibit the regulatory uses of individually identifiable data obtained for statistical purposes. In other words, the information you submit can be used against you by enforcement agencies.

Another problem is that the Act only loosely limits the exchange of identifiable individual information among agencies. The Act requires agencies to tell respondents of the anticipated routine uses of the information they submit. But it allows agencies to exchange identifiable information for unanticipated purposes if those purposes are consistent with the original purpose. The standards for defining consistent use are loose. [20] The report recommends that "statistical records across all federal agencies should be governed by a consistent set of statutes and regulations."

Perhaps not surprisingly, there is not yet a specific law on the books that truly protects an individual's privacy from the myriad modern-day intrusions by marketers, credit investigators, door-knocking activists soliciting funds, panhandlers, and polltakers, not to mention the government. Without this kind of protection, the public is likely to grow increasingly fearful and resentful of the census. And books such as *The Naked Consumer— How Our Private Lives Become Public Commodities* heighten public worries about these intrusions. [21]

Aware of the ground swell of public fear and resentment over the invasion of privacy, the newsletter *Privacy and American Business* forecasted in late 1993: "There will be an outpouring in the next three to five years of new privacy policies and procedures governing business uses of consumer (and employee) information. What will be critical for business—and for American society—in this process is how wisely reasonable expectations of privacy will be defined; whether information technology can help individual consumers decide how their information is used; and whether voluntary policies or detailed regulation play the dominant role in assuring consumer and employee privacy."[22]

Just as Watergate prompted the enactment of the Privacy Act of 1974, so too events and developments of recent years are provoking Congress, the courts, and the private sector to revisit the amorphous but pressing purview of privacy. The advent of the information highway—bringing disparate databases together and into the home or office via the TV and computer modem— holds great promise, but also dangers. Congress is now devising regulations in that arena.

During the 1992 presidential campaign, candidate Clinton criticized the Bush administration for its weak privacy record with regard to consumer protection and abortion rights. In discussing privacy and the abortion issue, candidate Clinton told interviewer Bill Moyers: "I am worried about the Bill of Rights and the right to privacy—not just the right to choose but the general right to privacy, which I think is very important." [23]

As president, Clinton has been the object of aggressive reporting not just about his leadership, but about his private life and personal finances. This has re-ignited heated arguments over the media's right to know, and the privacy rights of public officials.

Vice-President Gore's "reinventing government" report proposes to establish uniform privacy protection practices through a federal privacy protection board. [24] Privacy and confidentiality are on the front burner in the 1990s, with the building of the information highway. The intensity of the debate will grow as the countdown to census 2000 begins.

References

1. Pear, Robert (1994). "Federal Panel Proposes Register to Curb Hiring of Illegal Aliens," *The New York Times*, August 4, 1994, p. 1.

2. Lee, Laura Murphy (1994). "On the Sharing of Census Address Lists," Testimony before the Subcommittee on Census, Statistics, and Postal Personnel, Committee on Post Office and Civil Service, July 21, 1994, p. 14.

3. *Privacy and American Business* (1993). Vol. 1, No. 1, September/October 1993, p. 3.

4. Panel on Confidentiality and Data Access, Committee on National Statistics, Commission on Behavioral and Social Sciences and Education, National Research Council, Social Science Research Council (1993). *Private Lives and Public Policies* (Washington, D.C.: National Academy Press, 1993), p. 8.

5. Cassedy, James H. (1969) *Demography in Early America: Beginnings of the Statistical Mind, 1600-1800*, (Cambridge: Harvard University Press, 1969), p. 216.

6. *A Century of Population Growth* (Washington, DC: Government Printing Office, 1909), p. 48.

7. Bohme, Frederick G. and David M. Pemberton (1991). "Privacy and Confidentiality in the U.S. Censuses—A History," paper presented at the American Statistical Association, Atlanta, GA, August 18-22, 1991.

8. Proclamation for the Thirteenth Decennial Census, March 15, 1910.

9. Bohme and Pemberton, p. 9.

10. Anderson, Margo J. (1988). *The American Census: A Social History* (New Haven: Yale University Press, 1988), p. 243, table 3.

11. Cited in letter from E.R. Magie, acting solicitor, to the secretary of commerce, January 15, 1920.

12. Bohme and Pemberton, p. 1.

13. *Ibid*, p. 12.

14. *Ibid*, p. 12.

15. Title 13, United States Code Census. Prepared by the Committee on Post Office and Civil Service, United States Senate, December 31, 1976, plus amendments to Title 13 subsequent to December 31, 1976.

16. Greenberg, Brian (1990). "Disclosure Avoidance Research at the Census Bureau," *Proceedings, 1990 Annual Research Conference,* (Washington DC: Bureau of the Census, 1990).

17. Panel on Confidentiality and Data Access, pp. 111-115. Also: *The Privacy Act of 1974: An Assessment* (Washington, D.C.: U.S. Government Printing Office, 1977).

18. *Ibid*, p. 118.

19. Lee, p. 7.

20. Panel on Confidentiality and Data Access, pp. 132-133.

21. Larson, Erik (1992). *The Naked Consumer* (New York: Henry Holt and Company, 1992)

22. Westin, Alan F. and Robert R. Belair (1993). "Privacy & American Business' Editorial Policy," *Privacy & American Business,* Vol. 1, No. 1, September/October 1993, p. 2.

23. "Clinton, Privacy, and the Business Agenda," *Privacy & American Business*, Vol. 1, No. 1, September/October, 1993, p. 1.

24. Gore, Albert (1993). *From Red Tape to Results: Creating a Government That Works Better and Costs Less*, Report of the National Performance Review (New York: Times Books, 1993), p. 166.

CHAPTER 3

In the Crosshairs:
The Census Bureau and Its Director

When Bill Clinton was elected, he promised an administration that would "look like America," capturing the rich diversity of our nation's population. While he achieved that goal with many of his appointments, it slowed the appointment process considerably. The directorship of the Census Bureau was empty for nearly two years—22 months to be exact—after Clinton took office in January 1993 and I left the position. Finally, Dr. Martha Farnsworth Riche became my successor.

Because the Census Bureau is at the crosshairs of the growing public distrust of government and the national debate over privacy, to leave the bureau rudderless for that long further erodes public confidence in the government's important data-collection efforts. As the philosopher and all-star New York Yankee catcher Yogi Berra once observed: "It's like *déjà vu* all over again." This has happened before, but never before has the directorship been vacant for so long.

The directorship of the Census Bureau was vacant for 11 months before I assumed the position—just four short months before the start of the 1990 census. That, too, was eerily reminiscent of what happened a decade earlier. Months before the launch of the 1980 census, Emmanuel "Manny" Plotkin, the director who had been appointed by Jimmy Carter, resigned from the post. Scrambling to find a replacement who could hit the ground running, Carter was deluged with advice from assorted special-interest groups. He surprised many in April of 1979 by turning to Vincent Barabba, a marketing director at Xerox. Barabba had been the director of the Census Bureau during the second Nixon administration and through that of Gerald Ford. When he was first proposed for director in 1973 by President Richard Nixon, Barabba was criticized at his confirmation hearing by some academic researchers and opposed by the American Statistical Association. They feared the Census Bureau would be politicized because Barabba came from a Republican polling firm. Ironically, Barabba would be elected president of the American Statistical Association in 1992. Barabba proved the doubters wrong by resisting White House efforts to compromise the bureau during the Nixon administration. Welcomed the second time around by census staffers, Barabba would prove an outstanding and unflappable director of a difficult but ultimately successful census taken in an increasingly tumultuous environment.

The Census Bureau was once a low-profile agency, left alone to do what it does best. Now it is the focus of intense scrutiny and political pressure. Its professional staff struggles to maintain its independence, but that is difficult to do without a chief to run interference.

Until Detroit Mayor Coleman A. Young filed the first lawsuit against the Census Bureau on April 1, 1980, the bureau had never actually been sued for the undercount. Since then, it has been ensnared in at least 73 suits. This has created a bunker mentality at the bureau and even more so at the level of the Department of Commerce and its General Counsel's Office. There, winning lawsuits can take priority over the bureau's desire to have open and responsive communication with Congress, the press, and the public. This type of communication is critical at a time of growing public distrust.

"Now we figure we're going to be sued no matter what we do," said one of the bureau's assistant directors in a 1990 off-the-record interview with a *USA Today* reporter.

The stakes in modern American life have risen dramatically, spawning battles between population winners and losers. The Census Bureau is in the middle because it is dealing the cards— the census statistics that determine reapportionment and redistricting. The studiously non-partisan bureau is stuck in a rising political storm. The politicians want to count the people. The people increasingly want to be left alone. In this environment, the Census Bureau can't do anything right.

Reapportionment and redistricting, which are based on population shifts as quantified by the decennial census, have steadily moved Congressional seats and political clout to the South and West and to America's suburbs. After the 1980 census, 17 seats moved out of the Northeast and Midwest to the South and West. The 1990 census moved an additional 15 in the same direction, for a total of 32 among 435 seats in only 20 years.

The creation of minority-majority Congressional districts under the Voting Rights Act of 1965, burgeoning government programs, the funneling of federal funds back to communities, and actions taken to correct proliferating social problems are all dependent on census data.

But what if the numbers are wrong—or someone thinks they are? New York City, which lost population (and government funding) in the 1970s, believed the census count seriously understated its population, compounding its problems.

To prove its case, New York City's attorneys sought access to the bureau's confidential address lists in 1980. They wanted to check the lists against the city's own registers to spot missing housing units. A lower court agreed and ordered the bureau to turn over its lists. Director Barabba refused, insisting that the records were confidential and that turning them over would breach Title 13, damage public trust in the bureau, and jeopardize future census taking. Risking fines and jail, Barabba defied the lower court.

It was a watershed in the new political environment of colliding rights and needs, and a bold reassertion of the bureau's commitment to the confidentiality of census data. Ultimately the case reached the U.S. Supreme Court, which decided in the bureau's favor. Confidentiality ruled.

Nevertheless, New York City had a point. The census does not and cannot count everyone. How can the bureau improve the accuracy of the count and at the same time preserve the confidentiality of census records?

While Barabba was making his principled stand, he was also overseeing an internal study of the undercount problem and the feasibility of adjusting the census. Barabba was open to the possibility of adjustment if it would significantly improve the accuracy of census results. In the end, he recommended against adjusting the 1980 figures, finding the techniques unproven and with no guarantee of improving the results.

Not until 1987 were all of the lawsuits stemming from the 1980 census either thrown out by the courts or decided in the bureau's favor.

His job complete with the delivery of the 1980 results to the president, Barabba left the hot seat. He is now executive-in-charge of General Motors' Business Decision Center/Corporate Information Management. After running the Census Bureau twice and facing down more than four dozen lawsuits, Barabba with his easy smile figured that a global auto war would be a piece of cake.

The explosive matter of the undercount was far from settled and would resurface sooner than expected. Research on the undercount problem and techniques for correcting it continued at the bureau. Barabba was succeeded by Bruce Chapman, then by John G. Keane, both Reagan appointees. Keane wanted the results of undercount research to be the deciding factor on whether or not to adjust the 1990 census.

But the Commerce Department, of which the Census Bureau is a part, announced in late 1987 that there would be no 1990 adjustment. Among the reasons: "there are questions about the validity" of adjustment techniques, corrections were "unlikely to improve" on the count expected, efforts related to quantify the undercount and make an adjustment would "dilute resources" from other census operations.

The Commerce Department might as well have waved a red flag in front of census critics. It provoked New York City and its mayor, Edward Koch, to file suit in 1988, alleging that the inevitable undercount that would occur in the 1990 census would violate the Constitutional rights of the city's citizens because of the money and political representation they would lose as a result. The city sought to require statistical adjustment of the yet-to-be-taken census. This was but the first volley in a massive strike. The states of New York and California, the U.S. Conference of Mayors, the National League of Cities, the League of United Latin American Citizens, and the National Association for the Advancement of Colored People joined New York City—I suspect gleefully—as initial plaintiffs in the suit. The suit was referred to as New York et al. Eventually al. included 50 plaintiffs.

At the end of the Reagan Administration, Keane left the battlefield for reserved football seats at the University of Notre Dame, where he is now Dean of the College of Business Administration.

Plums and Prunes

The Plum Book, as it is called, lists 4,500 appointed positions in the federal government. Its title derives not from its official name nor from the color of the book's cover, which is actually canary yellow, but from the prestigious jobs like ambassadorships, cabinet posts, under secretaries, and assistant secretaries. These are considered plums and are dispensed by the political party occupying the White House. [1]

Then, there's *The Prune Book*. [2] Despite its waggish name, it's actually a factual tome, sponsored by the Carnegie Commission on Science, Technology, and Government, that describes "the 60 toughest science and technology jobs in Washington." These are jobs that no one in his or her right mind would want, much less accept. It's the successor to another book with the same name listing the "100 toughest management and policy-making jobs." [3]

Both the Plum and *Prune* books include: Director, Bureau of the Census, U.S. Department of Commerce. And, I wanted it! While it was a presidential, and therefore a political appointment, it was not the sort of spot into which a thankful president would put a top fund raiser—unlike an ambassadorship to Bermuda or to the Court of St. James. I volunteered to become a prune. Taking on tough assignments was not new to me, nor was arriving late in the game.

I knew my name was in the hat shortly after President Bush was elected in November 1988. I knew who put my name in the hat, and I had suggested that he do so. He was Robert M. Teeter, co-director of Bush's transition team, who had directed strategy research and polling for Bush's campaign. After the election of a non-incumbent president, a transition team begins to staff the incoming administration. The transition team's mandate runs from the day after the election until Inauguration Day, after which staffing decisions move into White House personnel operations.

Teeter was a former colleague at Market Opinion Research, where I was then a senior vice-president. He had been president of Market Opinion Research until he joined the Bush campaign in early 1988. Teeter and I had been associates since 1970 when he and Frederick P. Currier, Market Opinion Research's chairman, hired me to build up the non-political side of the company's survey research business. Teeter was busy expanding the company's business from a local to a national force in political research. But Teeter and Currier knew the company couldn't live on politics alone.

After Bush won the election, I called Bob to congratulate him and added casually: "While you're filling all those jobs, think about me for director of the Census Bureau—being sued doesn't faze me."

In a political patronage system, I knew I was an unlikely choice. I hadn't so much as stuffed an envelope for a political campaign. While a Republican philosophically, I wasn't formally registered on any party rolls because we don't register by party in Michigan. I had worked indirectly for three presidents, but one of them had been a Democrat. During my years at Market Opinion Research, I landed contracts for national research work for Gerald Ford's Commission on Observance of International Women's Year, for Jimmy Carter's Commission on World Hunger, and for Ronald Reagan's Commission on Americans Outdoors. Among survey researchers I was distinguished by these studies, and by having served for six years on one of the Census Bureau's professional advisory committees. I had fallen in love with the work the bureau does.

Furthermore, no woman had ever headed the census. But times were changing, and there had to be a first. Demographically, I was the quintessential mother of the baby-boom era, married to a veteran with the requisite three children. Mine was the generation of women who, after World War II, worked for a short time, then got married, had children, and stayed home. The problem for me was that home wasn't where the heart was, even with children and a husband whom I adored.

In my brief career before I married, I'd been one of the first women to gain the rank of editor at a McGraw-Hill technical magazine. I'd taken the chance offered to one person on each magazine to learn layout and typography so the company could improve the looks of its magazines. Being art editor of *Chemical Engineering* magazine wasn't practicing the physics I had studied. But the job did make me a bona fide editor just one year after I graduated from Cornell.

I left McGraw-Hill in 1948 to move to Illinois to marry John H. Bryant, then studying for a Ph.D. in electrical engineering. Our children, Linda, Randal, and Lois, followed in that order over the next seven years and we moved to Michigan. When Lois got on the school bus for first grade in 1961, the other mothers were tearfully wiping their eyes. I was dancing in the street!

The next day I started back to work at a local university, taking a part-time position that quickly turned into an underpaid full-time job.

While John supported my career, he eventually pointed out what was apparent to me after three-and-one-half years on the job: "You'll always be overworked and underpaid around a university if you only have a bachelor's degree." John didn't mind my working, but only if I did so first class. "You are underachieving, and it's not worth it for the family if you work that way," he said.

A comment by my boss hastened my departure for graduate school. Intending to compliment me, he offhandedly said one day: "For the salaries we pay, I can hire women who are much more qualified and capable than men." Now two men were telling me I was overworked and underpaid!

Being underpaid never happened to me again. I learned ten years before the dawn of the feminist movement—and I learned it from men—to demand equal pay.

Off I went to Michigan State University in East Lansing,

intending to get a master's degree so that I could earn promotions at the university from which I came. But I detoured when I discovered communication research, which combined two of my long-term interests—science and writing. This field introduced me to survey research.

Five years, 80,000 miles, and two Plymouths later, I had a Ph.D. I've always measured that degree in commuter miles rather than credit hours. I was 44 years old. I had a job offer from Market Opinion Research, where I would spend the next 19 years and from where I would call Bob Teeter at the transition team about my desire to be the director of the Census Bureau.

The transition team went out of existence on January 20, 1989, without naming a director. I soon forgot the idea. It had been an off-the-wall thought anyway, one that I never really expected to happen.

I now know what I didn't know then. If an enemy country ever wants to take over the United States, it should do so during the year after a new president is elected. Nobody's minding the store—or at least most of its counters.

Once the cabinet members are nominated and confirmed, the public doesn't pay much attention to whether the rest of the presidential appointees—deputy secretaries, under secretaries, assistant secretaries, and heads of major agencies—have been nominated by the president and confirmed by the Senate. No corporation runs that way.

The media wake up from time to time when a special-interest group points out that there is no one in charge of civil rights in the Justice Department, or whatever. They also wake up when there's a rumor as to who is to get a top job.

I also know now who plants the rumors. They are trial balloons launched by the new administration to reveal as much dirty linen as possible on potential nominees before the nomination is made.

In March of 1989 I got a call from Dr. Michael R. Darby, recently nominated as under secretary of economic affairs of the Commerce Department. "Are you still interested in the directorship of the Bureau of the Census? You're one of three finalists," he said.

Within days, I was in Washington. Darby interviewed me, then sent me for an interview with the secretary of commerce, Robert A. Mosbacher. I emerged from those meetings into a gorgeous spring day feeling like a winner. Both men had arranged a second interview with me—subtle indications were that I had moved to the top of the heap. Clearly, I was in serious contention.

I arranged a Sunday afternoon briefing with former Census Bureau director Vince Barabba, then in Detroit where I was. I consulted by phone with Jack Keane, the most recent ex-director, on the pitfalls and opportunities of the position. I knew both of them well because we had served together on the national board of the American Marketing Association in their pre-census days. Neither of them wanted to direct the Census Bureau again, but both agreed that being the director of the bureau was an experience they wouldn't have missed. I also met with Teeter and his administrative assistant. They wanted to be certain that I understood the danger of the terrain. They knew I was fairly tough, but wanted to be certain I realized how much tougher this was than anything I had ever faced at Market Opinion Research.

When I came back to Washington for the second interview nine days later, I talked only to Darby. There was no need to meet with Mosbacher because it seemed the California Congressional Republican delegation wanted their man to be the director. Their man was Alan Heslop—one of the other finalists—and they were pressuring the Administration to appoint him. I had no organized group of political sponsors with the clout of that Congressional delegation. California, because of its growth during the 1980s, would clearly have the most at stake in increased Congressional seats once the 1990 census was taken.

Soon after, a *Washington Post* article reported, "Alan Heslop, a California redistricting specialist closely associated over the years with Republican political planning, is the leading candidate to become director of the Census Bureau...Barbara Bryant, a vice president of Market Opinion Research, Robert Teeter's old polling firm, also has been a contender for the post, but apparently lost out to Heslop." [4]

Oh, well, I thought. It was an interesting experience just to have been considered for the position, and to almost make it. My ego wasn't bruised. The rumors planted and published in *The Washington Post* had separated out who had clout and who did not. I returned to my job at Market Opinion Research, taking on a huge new transit authority study.

Meanwhile, Heslop's name was flying high. But California Democrats were taking aim. The rumors were now working in the other direction. The Democrats did not want their opponent in the redistricting of California into salamander-shaped districts after the 1980 census to be in charge of collecting the data that would determine the next reapportionment.

In fact, the collection of census data is invulnerable to any political tampering. Census data are mailed directly to the bureau from individual households or they are gathered by the army of enumerators. The data go straight into computers, one household at a time, almost untouched by human hands. Still the California Democrats—presumably Willie Brown and the state assembly he controlled—did not want California Republican hands anywhere near the census data. Better Michigan Republican hands, even ones that had worked with the president's pollster.

Back in Michigan, I was oblivious to all this behind-the-scenes wrangling until one morning in late June when a fax arrived from Market Opinion Research's Washington office. "Candidate for Census Bows Out...Barbara Bryant is a contender," reported the faxed article from—where else?—*The Washington Post.* [5] Heslop had withdrawn his name from consideration, citing personal reasons. This was news to me. It was certainly news to Market Opinion Research. After the initial round of courtship, I had assured the company that I was staying put.

Three hours later I got an urgent phone call. It was Commerce Secretary Mosbacher. Would I come down and talk to him? Here we go again!

If being picked is a seven-month process, getting into office is even more arduous, marked by extensive financial and ethics disclosure statements and a total FBI check. The FBI asked me for four names as references. Little did I realize they would use those as network nodes from which to fan out.

"I was called by the FBI today," Beverly Beltaire, president of P/R Associates, a Detroit public relations firm, gleefully reported to me. Hers was not one of the names I had given the FBI. "They asked me if you live beyond your means," she said. "I told them: Don't we all?"

"Gee, thanks, Bev," I told her.

"I'm absolutely incensed about our government," said Marsha Sussman, Market Research Director of the National Geographic Society, when she called me in indignation. Hers was another name I had not given the FBI. National Geographic was a major client of Market Opinion Research and one for whom I'd directed several research projects.

"An FBI agent asked me whether you drink too much and whether you've ever used drugs. I said I didn't know, but I had never seen you do so," said Sussman. "But he never asked me whether you know anything about survey research...I think they cared more about whether you would make a good dope peddler than a good census director!"

I passed FBI muster. The job was finally mine—but without a title, office, or authority at first. There was only one last hurdle to clear—Senate confirmation hearings. While I waited, I was brought to Washington as a consultant. But I was not allowed to speak for the Census Bureau, sign anything on behalf of the Census Bureau, sit in the director's office, or even act like the presidential nominee I was about to become—those are every administration's rules prior to actual nomination and Senate confirmation.

The 1990 census operations were going into high gear and as director-to-be I was muzzled and frustrated. "Please, Senate, move fast," I thought, after the dawdling White House finally submitted my nomination papers on October 6.

It was already too late for me to change any of the operational plans for the 1990 census. By now I was aware that—although census logistics and operations were well and thoroughly planned—there were several things I would have changed if only I'd been in office a year earlier. I could still promote the meaning of the census and the importance of being counted. It takes time to get this concept across to the public, whose memory doesn't hark back ten years. But a headless Census Bureau couldn't get the attention it needed.

I wasn't the only one waiting. By November, 106 nominations were on the Hill awaiting confirmation. Some went as far back as June, mine only to October. But mine had a census waiting in the wings. According to *The Washington Times*, the White House blamed Senate Democrats for stalling; Senate Majority Leader George Mitchell of Maine fired back: "My review makes it clear that the principal cause of the delay is the administration itself." [6]

"Don't start the census without me," I fretted. I was due for a confirmation hearing before the Senate Committee on Governmental Affairs, chaired by Senator John Glenn, the Ohio Democrat and former astronaut. It never happened. The Senate left on its extended Christmas recess, which begins just before Thanksgiving.

With the clock ticking and census troops getting mighty anxious, President Bush used the presidential prerogative of a recess appointment to make me director in the absence of Senate hearings. The date: December 7, 1989, the 48th anniversary of the Japanese attack on Pearl Harbor.

By whatever maneuver, I was now Thomas Jefferson's successor (a hard act to follow) and the 31st director in 200 years of census taking. In a hasty ceremony that seemed like a shotgun wedding, I was given the oath of office by deputy secretary of commerce Thomas J. Murrin. The following summer, after the taking of the 1990 census, the Senate would confirm me and I would get the full dress swearing-in ceremony.

On that day in December, I swore the oath that binds me for the rest of my life not to use any information furnished to the Census Bureau in censuses or surveys for anything other than the statistical purpose for which the information is supplied. I also agreed not to publish any census information in which the data furnished by any particular establishment or individual could be identified. Any violation of these promises is subject to a fine of not more than $5,000 or imprisonment of not more than five years, or both. It's a tough oath under Title 13, even for she who wanted the job.

Meanwhile, Senator Glenn was reportedly miffed upon learning of my recess appointment. As reported by the Associated Press: "President Bush on Thursday took a parliamentary end run around the Senate to install a new census director whose nomination had been languishing." [7] It might not have been pretty or efficient, but it was official, and it was business as usual in Washington.

Washington is a power city in which only those nominated or elected have clout. The best of civil servants can't get the attention of the Congress in the way a presidential appointee can. Thus, despite all the warts in the appointment process, it is important that the director of the Census Bureau be a presidential appointee, confirmed by the Senate.

But the decennial census, the largest and certainly the most controversial of the many censuses and surveys undertaken by the Census Bureau, is out of phase with a four- or eight-year presidential cycle. Every 20 years, or every other census, a new administration is likely to come to power in the year just before the census. When this occurs, the director of the Census Bureau has less than one year by the time he or she has been chosen, nominated, and installed in office to prepare to direct the enormous census-taking operation. This is far too short a time. A much better system would be to appoint the census director for a five-year term, beginning in years ending in one and six. A director appointed by the president in the year ending in six, 1996 for example, would oversee the final testing and planning for the next census, and remain in office through delivery of the count. The director would be eligible for reappointment, but if the political winds had changed, a new director would be nominated the year following the decennial census. In this way, each director would also oversee one cycle of the every-five-year economic, agriculture, and government censuses, which are also conducted by the bureau.

Admittedly, this would sometimes mean that the Census Bureau's director would be a holdover from a previous administration. But since the Census Bureau itself is very consciously non-partisan, this would enhance the bureau's image in the public's perception. Perhaps a better image would boost public participation in the collective count, the census, which is so important to the well-being of our society.

References

1. *Policy and Supporting Positions*, a list of appointive positions published in the fall of each quadrennial election year (Washington, D.C.: U.S. Government Printing Office).

2. Trattner, John H. (1992). *The Prune Book: The 60 Toughest Science and Technology Jobs in Washington,* The Carnegie Commission on Science, Technology and Government (Lanham, Maryland: Madison Books, 1992).

3. Trattner, John H. (1988). *The Prune Book: The 100 Toughest Management and Policy-Making Jobs in Washington* (Lanham, Maryland: Madison Books, 1988).

4. Devroy, Ann and Spencer Rich (1989). "Californian May Take Next Census: Democrats Express Caution About Redistricting Expert Heslop," *The Washington Post*, April 26, 1989, p. A25.

5. Devroy, Ann (1989). "Candidate for Census Bows Out; Hill Democrats Opposed Confirmation," *The Washington Post*, June 23, 1989, p. A21.

6. Bedard, Paul (1989). "Bush mulls end run on nominees," *The Washington Times*, November 9, 1989, pp. A1, A8.

7. Associated Press, (1989). "Bush Names New Census Director," December 7, 1989.

CHAPTER 4

Why the Food Fight?

The census provides much of the fuel for our information-driven society. It rarely gets the credit it deserves, however. To the contrary, every few decades a handful of Congressional representatives suggest stripping back the decennial census to the simple population count called for in the Constitution. One of the reasons is to protect individual privacy; another is to cut costs.

What these advocates fail to realize is that a simple count would not be so simple. It would not provide highway planners with updated facts on commuting. It would not provide the Veterans Administration with the information it needs to plan and deliver medical services to veterans. It would not tell states and local school districts how many preschoolers will soon enter their classrooms. It would not provide meaningful consumer information to entrepreneurs who create jobs.

In the 1960s, Ohio Congressman Jackson Betts challenged expanding the census questionnaires as an invasion of privacy. "Going beyond the mandatory purpose of counting the population for Congressional districts is an abuse of federal power," he said. [1] Answering the census was then, and still is, mandatory. Betts introduced a bill (it never passed) to make it voluntary to answer any census questions that were not on the 1790 census. His opponents defended the additional questions, and their successors do today, because they provide essential data on the demographic and socioeconomic characteristics of Americans.

A debate between census advocates and those who wish to scale back the count takes place every few years. That debate is raging today. The chief proponents of a stripped-down census were the chair and the ranking minority member of the Subcommittee of Commerce, State, and Justice of the House Committee on Appropriations. Their rationale was to reduce the cost of census 2000. During my tenure at the bureau and in the Congress immediately following, Representative Neal Smith of Iowa (D) headed this committee and Harold Rogers of Kentucky (R) was the ranking minority member. They controlled the Census Bureau's purse strings. They jerked the purse strings closed in 1994, cutting funding for planning the 1995 test census to just one-third the original amount. Ironically, the goals of the test census—to experiment with ways to cut census costs—were the same as the goals Smith and Rogers espouse. Finally recognizing this, they loosened up on the purse strings for fiscal 1995.

Representative Rogers has suggested that the U.S. Postal Service could take the census. He thinks mail carriers could collect census data by working extra weekend hours because, in his words, "carriers know everyone on their routes." The carriers in his rural district of Kentucky probably do. Not so in New York City and other densely populated places as Representative Charles Schumer so frequently points out. New York is not like rural Kentucky, nor are the other big cities of the nation.

Between Representative Betts in the 1960s and Representatives Smith and Rogers recently lies the shared feeling that the census has grown far too costly and invasive of people's privacy. But 40 years of Congressional actions by their peers in Congress make a 1790-style head count impossible. Various federal laws require asking Americans, at a minimum, their age, sex, race, Hispanic origin, and relationship to the householder. The laws require asking a sample of people about their education, place of birth, citizenship, the year they came to the United States if foreign born, the language they speak, and their income. They require asking householders whether they own or rent their housing unit. And they require asking a sample of householders how many rooms are in their home, the year the structure was built, and whether it is on a farm.

"Why should I give the government all this information?" asked one of my middle-class friends after receiving the long form of the 1990 census questionnaire. She confronted me as the personal embodiment of the U.S. government.

"Why do you need to know where I work, whether I drive a car to work, and whether anyone rides with me?" she went on. "I'm willing to be counted, but whether someone rides with me is none of your business. Besides," she continued, "I don't need any government handouts!"

"Do you drive to work?" I asked, knowing full well that every member of my friend's family over the age of 16 had a car.

"Chances are the highway you use was placed there because of the answers to questions like these on earlier censuses. Those answers showed where roads were needed," I told her. "And if you rode a bus to work, the bus route was planned using the same information."

Clearly, my friend, like many others, assumed that the government collects information only to provide what she considers government handouts.

In fact, census results are indispensable to both the public and private sectors—they are used by local governments for planning, by businesses for marketing, and by the federal government in formulae for distributing funds. No retailer decides where to put a new store, mall, or restaurant without reviewing the size and characteristics of the local population. Population counts also determine sites for schools, parks, and hospitals.

Congress has written laws that make census counts, or the annual population estimates based on census counts, all or part of the formulae for allocating nearly $150 billion to about 120 different programs each year. [2] My friend might describe some of these programs as handouts, but many people would disagree. All of the programs funnel federal tax money back to the states and localities where it came from—money for which governors and mayors fight tooth and nail. And this $150 billion does not include any of the monies from state sales or income tax that are distributed to counties and local communities according to population counts.

Only a small part of the $150 billion changes hands due to shifts in population, because many other factors are also part of these formulae. But enough money changes hands to provoke a crisis over census counts every ten years.

Among the 120 federal programs that receive money based in part on population counts, 19 distributed over $1 billion in 1992. The biggest pot is Medicaid Title XIX—worth $70 billion in fiscal 1992. Medicaid dollars are divided among the states by a formula that includes the ratio of the state's per capita income to U.S. per capita income as one of its factors. To determine this ratio, government analysts divide income figures from the Bureau of Economic Analysis by the most current population counts. In census years, this is the actual census count. For the years between censuses, it is the Census Bureau's estimates of state populations, which are updates of census counts.

After Medicaid, the biggest sum is the $18 billion for highway planning and construction (Federal Aid Highway Program). The government's formulae for distributing this money are based on state shares of urban and rural populations. This is the money that brings you traffic jams on the interstates during the warm-weather months. Be prepared to slow down, because states will be getting huge sums for constructing and rehabilitating the interstate highway system over the next few years, all based in part on census data.

The states also divvied up $14 billion earmarked for Aid to Families with Dependent Children in 1992. Of this amount, $6 billion goes to local schools to help children from poor families attain grade-level proficiency. The decennial census counts the children and measures their family income. Some $2 billion goes to Head Start, the pre-school program, and another $4 billion supports foster care and community development block grants.

The billions of dollars, distributed at least in part according to census counts, also pay for the acquisition of recreational land and facilities, for highway safety, job training, employment services, adoption assistance, housing programs, and airport improvements. They fund the Cooperative Extension Program, help those with drug and alcohol problems, assist crime victims, promote the arts, provide food for soup kitchens, and support literacy and other education programs.

In answering the census, we the people of the United States trade a small portion of our privacy for the many services provided by our government.

The Job Machine

As the battle rages between privacy advocates, cost cutters, and census boosters, the private sector grows increasingly concerned. The Census Bureau provides most of the demographic information used by businesses nationwide, either directly or in more palatable, repackaged versions sold by private data companies. Businesses worry when Congress wants to drop questions from the census questionnaire. They worry about cost cutting that could reduce the value of census data.

The census provides us with jobs—an appropriate end result of an agency that is part of the U.S. Department of Commerce. Census information is used by businesses to plan the products and services we need. As businesses succeed, they create jobs. The business use of censuses (population, economic, and agriculture) and other survey data has transformed our world, most often for the better.

• Census data alerted the nation's colleges to a potential drop in enrollments in the 1990s because the small baby-bust generation (or Generation X) was entering its late teens and early 20s. Thanks to census information, colleges knew they did not need to downsize dramatically because this age group would begin to grow again by the late 1990s as the children of the baby-boom generation (the baby boomlet) mature.

• Census data alerted businesses to the need to adapt their products to an aging population. Lee and Levi-Strauss, which outfitted the baby-boom generation in its youth, now offer fuller cut jeans to accommodate the expanding waistlines of middle-aged Americans.

• Census data help American businesses compete with their foreign rivals by revealing important market segments among American consumers—such as Generation X, today's young adults. Using demographic data, Chrysler designed the sporty and inexpensive Neon, introduced in January 1994, to compete with Japanese cars that are popular among this age group.

• Innovative entrepreneurs use census data to target areas with Black, Hispanic, and Asian consumers to sell them cosmetics, snack foods, toys, television programming, and even financial products. Now following their lead, major companies are beginning to pay attention by tailoring products and advertising to these segments of the population, whose numbers are growing proportionately much faster than the overall U.S. population.

• Companies searching for a good location to open a new plant or retail store closely scrutinize census data, particularly the detailed data on the nation's metropolitan areas.

• Direct mailers, who send households catalogs, advertising fliers, and envelopes crammed with coupons, combine neighborhood income and household data from the census with other information gleaned from credit card purchases, mortgage applications, and magazine subscriptions to determine who gets what. Census data can point catalog companies to neighborhoods with likely customers for toys or women's clothing. They reveal which neighborhoods direct mailers should target with discount coupons for things like travel packages.

While some may object to the business use of census and other demographic data on privacy grounds, this use of census data contributes greatly to American prosperity. The households targeted by businesses actually buy the advertised products; if they didn't, the mailings would cease.

The Feeding Frenzy

No wonder census counts create a feeding frenzy between governors and mayors. Each wants to maximize his or her share of the pie. Each wants to improve the odds of attracting the next Saturn, Honda, or BMW manufacturing plant. Localities across the country go to great lengths to ensure that all of their people are counted.

Rocky Mount, North Carolina, whose population jumped by 21 percent during the 1980s, hoped its rapid growth would propel it into the big-leagues—the ranks of metropolitan areas. When preliminary 1990 census results—sent during a process called local review before all counting operations were finished—suggested that Rocky Mount might just miss the population cutoff, local officials and the Chamber of Commerce swung into action, petitioning the bureau to review its numbers. In fact, once counting was complete, Rocky Mount made the cut with a metro population of 135,000. This meant it would forever after rank among the nation's metropolitan areas, which are targeted by businesses looking for new areas of opportunity.

Following the 1990 census, Washington, D.C., sued the Census Bureau over its count. At issue was the way the bureau counted prisoners. Washington, D.C.'s prison is in Lorton, Virginia. The Census Bureau includes the prisoners in Virginia's population. No protest from Virginia over that one!

Massachusetts sued the Census Bureau because it assigns overseas military, federal employees, and their dependents to the state that each has designated as his or her "home of record." In 1990, the difference in the overseas count between the states of Massachusetts and Washington was just enough to tip the allocation of the 435th congressional seat away from Massachusetts and to Washington.

The Census Bureau won both the Washington, D.C., and Massachusetts lawsuits, winning the Massachusetts suit in the Supreme Court. But defending the suits took the time of key personnel at the Census Bureau, at the Department of Commerce, and the Justice Department. Defending the suits also cost the taxpayers a lot of money.

With so much riding on census counts, many localities claim their constituencies are undercounted. But so far none has been able to prove in court that its own numbers are more accurate than those the census provides. Tax records, voter registration rolls, school enrollments, and other local data miss some of the country's residents. It is the census that comes the closest to including everyone. In addition, only the Census Bureau's own undercount estimates provide clues to the numbers and characteristics of those missed by the census.

Even those suing the Census Bureau know that its data are the best. In the midst of the New York City et al. suit against the bureau, a contract requiring a signature crossed my desk. New York City was contracting with the Census Bureau to do its vacancy survey, determining how many empty housing units the city had. Yet at the same time, the city was claiming in court that the bureau didn't know how to count!

The Power Machine

As if billions of dollars weren't enough, the census also determines who gets political power. It is the basis for reapportionment at the federal, state, and local levels.

The 435-seat House of Representatives is the biggest power pie. Imagine that it is a cherry pie. Each state gets one cherry automatically. After those 50 cherries are apportioned, the rest are divided up according to population counts (and none of the cherries can be split). The result is a substantial shift in political representation each decade: 19 House seats changed hands on the basis of the 1990 census, with a net of 15 moving South and West.

Congress adopted the formula for apportioning representatives among the states in 1941. Twice, the apportionment method has been deemed the fairest of several options by committees of the National Academy of Science.

After the number of cherries per state is announced following each census, the states must then determine the boundaries of each Congressional district. They must follow a 1962 Supreme Court decision (Baker vs. Carr and decisions since) once called "one man, one vote." The gist of it is this: within a state, Congressional districts must be as nearly equal in population as possible. With the help of computers to array population block by block, near equality is achievable, as long as no one minds districts with bizarre shapes. So far, the Supreme Court has said nothing about the shape of districts.

Census counts are also used to distribute power within each state, county, town, city, or village. At each legislative level, "one person, one vote" means equal-size districts. At the state and local level, again, there are no rules regarding district shapes.

This is a problem for Representative Melvin Watt (D) of North Carolina. When he's back home trying to stay in touch with his constituents, he spends much of his time in a car trying to find them. His 12th District meanders 160 miles in a serpentine pattern from north to southwest along I-85. That's roughly the distance from Baltimore to Atlantic City. But for long stretches, the district is not much wider than an interstate highway.

"If you drive down the interstate with both car doors open, you'd kill most of the people in the district," one pol joked.

This is one of the most extreme of several new districts crafted after the 1990 census to ensure a majority of Blacks, in accordance with the Voting Rights Act of 1965. It was so extreme that the U.S. District Court in Raleigh, North Carolina, acknowledged it as a "racial gerrymander," but ruled it nonetheless constitutional because it helps remedy past discrimination against Blacks. This 1994 ruling came after the U.S. Supreme Court handed the case back to the District Court with the directive to examine again claims by plaintiffs that White voters had been denied equal protection under the law. [3]

North Carolina's 12th District is not the only oddly shaped application of the Voting Rights Act, all subject to court review. Louisiana's fourth district borders 600 miles of the state, from Arkansas to Mississippi. Along the Mississippi River, it is only 85 feet wide in some places. Intended to end race-based voting discrimination, the Voting Rights Act requires the creation of districts with Black or Hispanic majorities or substantial minorities. It also requires the creation of districts for other non-White groups, when possible.

There are now 52 Congressional districts configured as a result of the Voting Rights Act: 32 Black, 18 Hispanic, and 2 Asian and Pacific Islander (both in Hawaii). This is twice the number of minority-majority districts as there were in 1980. In the 103rd Congress, the first after the 1990 reapportionment, 69 Congressional seats were held by minorities. This means that some majority-White districts elected representatives who were of other racial or ethnic groups

Redistricting is a once-a-decade bloodletting. In the old days, the two major political parties in each state would each draw up their own redistricting plans. What happened next varied from state to state, based on the rules, but usually included plenty of horse trading between the parties. Ultimately, the state legislature would have to pick one plan, usually the one that favored the majority party.

Redistricting controversies were strictly partisan until the Voting Rights Act. Even after its passage, the law was applied only to certain states, mostly those in the former Confederacy. In the 1980s, however, the Act was made applicable to all states, not just those with proven records of voting discrimination. This is why the impact of the Voting Rights Act was far greater following the 1990 census than at any time previously.

In the pre-computer days, state politicians would adjourn to back rooms (undoubtedly smoke-filled in those days) with tabulators, maps, and crayons and piece together district maps on the floor. The politicians literally taped together bits of paper representing blocks or voting precincts in various configurations until the right mix was achieved.

It was a slow, exclusive, process that discouraged most citizens or special-interest groups from getting involved. Felt-tip pens were the new technology after the 1960 census. By 1980, mainframe computers made it possible for the well-funded state Republican and Democratic parties to replace their tabulators and felt-tip pens with computer databases.

In 1980, the Connecticut Assembly contracted with my

former firm, Market Opinion Research of Detroit, to create an interactive database of census statistics and maps. This database included voting results for the past four elections, obtained from the state of Connecticut, and boundaries of the existing voting districts in the state, laboriously digitized to their latitudes and longitudes by Market Opinion Research. Each political party had its own workspace in two stone-lined rooms in the bowels of the Victorian-era Capitol building in Hartford. Each room was equipped with computer terminals and staffed by a trainer who explained to the politicians how to manipulate the database.

Each political party could access the database, which was linked to a big Michigan MTS computer system some 700 miles away. Neither party could see the other party's plans until one party chose to share its plan with the other. When one party did solicit an opinion from the other party, the typical reaction was, "Are you kidding?" Finally, the two parties managed to agree on the redistricting of Connecticut for the 1980s.

Connecticut wasn't the only state that went high-tech after the 1980 census, but it may have been the only one in which the two parties entered into a joint agreement with a contractor to determine redistricting. In other states, Republicans contracted with Market Opinion Research or the Rose Institute in California to help them redistrict. Democrats used Election Data Services in Washington, D.C., and other consulting firms. These contracts all required big bucks, costing from $150,000 for Connecticut to nearly half a million dollars for Michigan Republicans. Behind these high prices was the exorbitant cost of mainframe computer time.

Everything changed after the 1990 census. Redistricting is no longer the province of the big guys. Anyone can play the redistricting game, and several hundred have done so. The governors and majority and minority leaders in the legislatures of each state got all the needed data and maps from the Census

Bureau at no cost to the state. For everyone else the price of entry was less than $700 for any person, organization, or party with a personal computer (about $500 for a CD-ROM reader and $150 for state redistricting data on CD-ROM from the Census Bureau). Those who wanted to manipulate maps paid somewhat more for TIGER map files from the Census Bureau (already digitized with voting district boundaries), available for the first time, and contractor-supplied geographic information system (GIS) software.

The democratization of the redistricting game occurred because of personal computers, CD-ROMs, and TIGER. Now anyone can use these tools to devise a redistricting plan to further his or her interests. As a result, state legislatures were bombarded with alternative plans, not only from Democrats and Republicans, but from organized labor, Black and Hispanic groups, and others.

North Carolina reviewed 2,000 redistricting plans before the Department of Justice agreed to the outlines of the 12th District and another Black majority district whose boundaries make a Rorschach ink blot look organized.

Glen Newkirk, a North Carolina legislative official who oversaw his state's redistricting, slogged through every one of the 2,000 plans. Afterwards, he sent me a note of thanks for the bureau's help in getting data to his state promptly. "It is one of the few times in my life I have been able to give someone a gift of what has been called rare, abstract art in appreciation for their assistance." he wrote. [4] The "art" in question was a map of North Carolina's new districts, including the 12th.

The Voting Rights Act, coupled with greater access to census data, represents a giant leap forward in the fair representation of racial and Hispanic groups. At the same time, it has raised the possibility that we will Balkanize the nation, creating voting blocs of "have nots" pitted against voting blocs of "haves."

North Carolina's 12th District went to the Supreme Court because five White voters brought suit, charging that the design was unconstitutional and violated the redistricting principles of compactness and contiguousness.

Louisiana has a case brought by Ed Adams, a Black city councilman who sued to overturn Louisiana's districts because they promote a segregated society. A federal court agreed and eliminated a majority Black district in Louisiana on the basis of racial gerrymandering. Shortly after the North Carolina decision upholding its two majority Black districts, including the 160-mile-long 12th, a three-judge panel struck down two districts in the Houston area and one in Dallas, Texas. [5] With federal judges and district courts coming up with conflicting decisions, the issue is bound to go to the Supreme Court.

Fairer representation may have in it the seeds of a divisive future. From the earmuff-shaped district outside of Chicago to the block-by-block jigsaw of Hispanic and Black districts in Queens, New York, gerrymandering has been raised to a new art form. The Founding Fathers must be writhing in their graves. In the short run the Voting Rights Act may be necessary, as the District Court in North Carolina ruled, to bring Congress closer to reflecting the rainbow of colors that now exists in the United States.

In the long run, this kind of redistricting may limit the number of Black and Hispanic representatives. It will create a few districts with majority concentrations rather than more districts with large minority populations, where candidates of all races and ethnicities are competitive.

The coupling of census data with computer technology has increased the power and importance of demographic information in general and of the census in particular. On the one side are those who believe the Census Bureau asks too much of the public too intrusively and at too much cost. On the other side are those who know that without the most accurate count possible, our nation will lack the information it needs to progress into the 21st century.

It should be apparent which side I am on. Getting the most accurate census count possible is of vital importance to all Americans. But we must face facts: the Census Bureau has done all it can to improve head counting. Because our population is becoming increasingly diverse, the task of counting only gets harder and more costly. The Census Bureau will not be able to do any better in 2000 than it did in 1990, when it achieved 98 percent net accuracy. Yet for many critics, this isn't good enough.

There is a better way. The Census Bureau could improve the accuracy of the count, cut costs, and be less intrusive of people's privacy if it were permitted to use statistical techniques on top of direct enumeration to count our nation's residents. Statistically estimating those missed by the census, and those avoiding the census, will help to control costs and ultimately provide better numbers for the many users of census data. It may also help quell the concerns of privacy advocates by giving those who wish to avoid direct enumeration a way out.

References

1. Lambert, Bruce (1993). "Jackson Betts, Congressman Who Criticized Census, Is Dead," *The New York Times*, April 15 1993, p. 44.

2. Tabulation by Barbara Everitt Bryant from an unpublished document of the Population Estimates Branch, Population Division, Bureau of the Census, "Federal Uses of Population Statistics," September 1, 1993. This unpublished report lists 119 formula grant programs that use population counts produced by the Census Bureau, either from the decennial census or from intercensal population estimates based on the census, as at least some part of the formulae for distribution of federal program funds. The total amounts distributed under these programs in fiscal 1992 were $148,470,000,000. The rounded $150 billion figure used in this book is far greater than any previously published. In September 1990 the General Accounting Office produced a report, *Federal Formula Programs: Outdated Population Data Used to Allocate Most Funds* (GAO/HRD-90-145), which referenced a prior publication, *Grant Formulas: A Catalog of Federal Aid to States and Localities* (GAO/HRD-87-28). The 1990 report showed only 93 programs distributing $27.5 billion in federal formula funds. In an analysis included as part of the report of under-secretary of commerce Michael Darby to the secretary of commerce in June 1991, Michael Murray of Bates College in Maine, pointed out that most federal formula programs are fixed pies; because of multi-factors in the formulae, allocations are not proportional to population size.

3. Smothers, Ronald (1993). "U.S. District Court Upholds 'Gerrymander' for Blacks," *The New York Times*, August 3, 1994, p. A8.

4. M. Glenn Newkirk, letter to Dr. Barbara Bryant, April 9, 1992.

5. "Texas: 3 congressional districts ruled illegal," *The Ann Arbor News*, August 18, 1994, p. A3.

CHAPTER 5

Launching a Census

Taking a census is a costly and complex operation. As we build the information highway, head counting is beginning to seem old-fashioned. Couldn't we do something more high-tech, some people ask, like combine all the administrative records already collected by the government?

In fact, some of the world's nations do just this. Countries such as Denmark and the Netherlands no longer take population censuses. According to Jan Carling, director general of Statistics Sweden, the 1990 census might be Sweden's last. [1] In the future, Statistics Sweden plans to use administrative records combined with the population registry and sample surveys to keep track of its people and their characteristics. Many countries require their citizens to register their names, addresses, and other information with the government. Centralized statistical bureaus then combine registry information with administrative records, sometimes supplementing the data with survey information.

The United States does not have this option, or at least the option has been vigorously resisted to date. Americans would not accept a population registry in which they would have to register their names and addresses with the government. And privacy advocates strongly resist any attempt by the government to track population change through administrative records, such as combining Social Security data with IRS files.

Because privacy is so important to Americans, the only way to learn what we need to know about ourselves is to count heads with a census. In fact, such an enumeration is required by the Constitution. No other country has kept its census going continuously for as long as the United States, with 21 censuses now under our belt. And no other nation takes as much time to count heads as we do, not even China with over 1 billion people, nor India with 800 million.

So far, census taking in the U.S. has worked. For 200 years, the government has convinced nearly everyone to respond to the census. That's not the case in many countries, nor is it likely to be so easy in this country in the future.

Nigeria has had a particularly sorry experience with census taking. It tried to take censuses in 1962 and again in 1963—its first since gaining independence from Britain in 1960. The results of both censuses were heatedly disputed and then altered by politicians who did not like what the results meant for the allocation of revenue and for electoral representation—the same things we fight about here. Unfortunately, Nigeria's government does not have a politician-proof census like we do. Despite our disagreements about census costs and procedures, even the president cannot change census numbers without proof that changing them would improve their accuracy.

Nigeria made a third try in 1973. The government nullified those results on the grounds that in many areas the counts appeared to have been inflated. On the next try, in 1989, Nigeria's military government took dictatorial action. It closed the country's borders, shut shops and factories, and ordered tens of millions of people to stay home for a week until they were counted. Nearly 700,000 census workers crisscrossed the African nation using Land Rovers, horses, donkeys, and canoes. This time the government succeeded at counting the population, finding a total of 88,514,501—a figure that is considerably less than the guesstimates of 95.7 million by the United Nations Population Division in 1985 or the mid-1988 estimate of 105 million by the World Bank. [2,3]

In the former Yugoslavia, the more people an ethnic group has, the greater its power. When the government of Macedonia attempted to take a census in 1994, following the breakup of Yugoslavia, the Serbs living there (who numbered 44,000 in a 1991 census) said they were 400,000 strong. Overall, Slavic Macedonians claimed to be 60 percent of the population, ethnic Albanians 40 percent (up from 21 percent in the 1991 census), Serbs 20 percent, not to mention smaller groups. [4] There's no undercount problem in Macedonia!

In a democracy like the United States, the government cannot order people to stay at home until they are counted, as Nigeria did. Census taking is a delicate operation, requiring just the right balance between government friendliness and force. In many countries, the government isn't so permissive. China, for example, requires everyone to register with the Ministry of Public Security. When it conducted its 1990 census, it reassigned 6 million government employees and retirees to take the count. Each enumerator started with the population register for 50 to 70 households. In urban districts, such as in Shanghai, residents were required to report to neighborhood census stations to complete their forms. Following a pre-canvas two weeks before the census to update the register, the actual counting was completed in an astounding ten days, according to State Statistical Bureau officials with whom I met in Beijing. The total: 1.13 billion. [5]

The questions asked by China's census are much like those asked by our census, except that China also asks how many babies women have had in six-month intervals for the past one and one-half years. The answers to this question are used to monitor whether families are adhering to the nation's one child per family population control policy. The Chinese government is not concerned about invading anyone's privacy nor does it offer even a pretense of confidentiality. "There's no need to keep the answers confidential," I was told. "The neighborhood workers already know the answers for the people in their neighborhood." John Paul Jones never raised his "don't tread on me" flag in China, nor would the mayor of Shanghai think of suing the State Statistical Bureau for an undercount.

It's not as easy to take a census in the United States where privacy is prized, antipathy to government is a given, and unlike China the population is in constant motion. On any given day, some 3.6 million people are traveling on business or vacation. Almost half of us (47 percent) live at an address different from the one we lived at five years earlier. Complicating the job further is the fact that some 2,200 legal immigrants enter the country every day, along with an estimated 500 to 600 illegal immigrants.

The High-Tech Census

One day in 1989, just after I became the director of the Census Bureau, I stood at the loading docks of the Census Bureau's Data Processing Division in Jeffersonville, Indiana. This is the bureau's largest facility outside of the Washington, D.C., area. It is where one-fifth of the bureau's permanent employees work. The space is vast, with building after building stretching over several acres.

The Jeffersonville property—or J-ville, as it is called at the bureau—was the site of the quartermaster depot that equipped the Union Army over 130 years ago. The history is appropriate because every ten years Jeffersonville becomes the site for gathering and dispersing the supplies to equip a civilian army of census takers.

As we prepared to launch the 1990 census, we used 850,000

square feet of working and storage space at Jeffersonville to receive, store, assemble, perform quality control, and ship 26 million pounds of paper and office equipment. Between censuses, the Census Bureau occupies only the space it needs at Jeffersonville for its ongoing mail-survey operations and the economic and agricultural censuses.

Unlike the 1860s, the buildings are now equipped with laser sorters, bar code scanners, microfilm processors, and high-speed readers that scan completed census questionnaires into computers.

These are but the latest inventions in a long tradition of innovation at the Census Bureau. Despite the drabness of the buildings housing the bureau, both at headquarters and Jeffersonville, and despite its reputation as a numbers factory, the bureau itself is a hotbed of high-tech creativity born of necessity. Many of the bureau's technological developments helped to make the information highway possible.

Between 1790 and 1880, census results were tabulated manually and laboriously, much like counting jellybeans in a jar. But after the 1880 census, there were too many jellybeans to count by hand. It took until 1887 to tabulate and publish the 1880 census—which at that time included questions on economic and agricultural activity, as well as population and housing characteristics. Not only had the population grown 30 percent in the decade since the last census, but there were 200 different census forms with 13,000 different questions. [6,7,8,9,10]

The 1890 census could not be tabulated with existing manual methods. That was the conclusion reached by Herman Hollerith, who worked at the Census Office (as it was then called) from 1879 to 1884 collecting statistics on the consumption of steam and water power by the iron and steel industry, and John Billings, physician in charge of compiling health statistics on loan to the

Census Office from the Surgeon General's Office. They thought that machines needed to be, and could be, developed to perform the mechanics of tabulating data.

After he left the government, Hollerith adapted punch cards so that holes in them could be counted by machines. He designed the pantograph punch and the electric tabulating machine, creating the first data-processing system. At age 28, Hollerith received his first order for the system from the Surgeon General's Office (probably due to his connection with Billings). Robert Porter, superintendent of the census, ordered six tabulating machines, plus their maintenance. The order was later expanded to 105. By using Hollerith's equipment, the Census Office was able to complete tabulating most of the 1890 census within three years. And then what happened? According to Hollerith's grandson, Richard Hollerith, the Census Office returned all 105 machines to Hollerith in 1894.

Struggling financially, Hollerith landed contracts in 1895 with both the Russian and French governments for their censuses and with the New York Central Railroad. [11] The following year, he formed the Hollerith Tabulating Company to manufacture machines and sell punch cards. [12] The Census Office used Hollerith's equipment to tabulate the 1900 census. As that census was ending, Hollerith invented automatic card feeders, boosting processing speed from about 10,000 to 84,000 cards a day. In 1905, after Hollerith's first patents had run out, the Census Bureau started building its own Hollerith-type equipment. [13] In 1911, Hollerith merged his expanding company with several others that were making time clocks, scales, and grinders. The result of the merger grew rapidly and prospered. In 1924 it became IBM.

Six censuses later, the Census Bureau was the first non-military organization in the U.S. to own an electronic computer. In 1946, officials at the Census Bureau started talking to computer pioneers J. Presper Eckert and John Mauchly about their computing needs. By law, the Census Bureau could not enter into a research and development contract. Instead, the bureau transferred $300,000 to the National Bureau of Standards, which let a contract for $75,000 to draw up the specifications. By May 1947, Eckert and Mauchly had named the proposed computer UNIVAC (Universal Automatic Computer). By the end of 1948, they had incorporated the Eckert-Mauchly Computer Corporation to raise more money than the Census Bureau could provide. By 1950, the company was nearly bankrupt. Eckert and Mauchly then sold it to Remington-Rand. UNIVAC I was delivered to the Census Bureau on March 31, 1951, in time to do some of the final processing of the 1950 census. [14,15]

There are two lessons to be learned from the stories of Hollerith, Eckert, and Mauchly: one, work with the Census Bureau if you want to start a data-processing revolution; two, don't expect the revolution to be profitable, at least not for a long time.

Computers are not the only technological innovation to emerge from census taking. Another was FOSDIC, or Film Optical Sensing Device for Input to Computer. M. Leighton Greenough of the National Bureau of Standards invented FOSDIC, which scanned microfilm of the 1960 questionnaires and transferred the answers onto computer tape. The fourth generation of FOSDIC, developed by bureau employee Paul Friday for the 1990 census, uses laser beams to read more than 1,300 questionnaire pages per minute into the computer. But Greenough continues to monitor his brainchild, as I learned when I dropped in on the FOSDIC laboratory in early 1990 and found him examining the new generation FOSDIC with Friday. "The physics behind his device has survived 40 years of competitive technological advances," Friday says of Greenough.

The Census Bureau is not allowed to patent or copyright its inventions. This is fortunate for the public, which gets the technological spin-off from the tax dollars it invests in the census. In fact, every century the census gives the nation a big birthday present, important technological innovations that have transformed our society from its agricultural roots to the information age of today. In 1790, the innovation was the census itself, which has provided the data that contributes to the growth of our nation as a free-market economy. In 1890 it was data processing, which grew into the computer industry. In 1990, it was TIGER.

TIGER is an acronym for Topologically Integrated Geographic Encoding and Referencing system. It is a powerful computer-mapping database that has turned geographic information systems (or GIS) technology into a major industry and business tool. The TIGER database includes the digitized boundaries of the 7 million blocks into which the Census Bureau divides the country. It includes the street names and address ranges on each block, as well as highways, secondary roads, rivers and railroads, and latitudes and longitudes of every point. [16] Every commercial geographic information system now uses TIGER as its base for drawing maps of the United States.

With TIGER, the Census Bureau automatically composed and printed multiple copies of over 1.3 million unique, detailed maps for use in the 1990 census. Today thousands of users extract their own maps from the TIGER database, downloading them into their own computers. They pay the Census Bureau only for the cost of reproduction of CD-ROM disks or tape.

TIGER is a tool for spatial analysis, allowing users to combine maps with census or other data. It is used extensively by government agencies and businesses. Rather than scan a long column of income statistics, for example, TIGER allows users to generate maps that differentiate neighborhoods by their income levels. Before TIGER, such maps had to be drawn laboriously by hand. Now computers can print them in a few minutes.

Many cities use TIGER to compute the shortest routes in response to 911 calls. Utilities plot their utility lines on TIGER maps. Trucking and delivery companies use TIGER to determine the most efficient routes. Marketers use TIGER to define market areas, then add census data to reveal the socioeconomic characteristics of potential customers.

TIGER development was kicked off in 1981 when Stanley Matchett, head of the bureau's Geography Division and a manager who could cut the mustard anywhere, assembled a team to analyze the problems of taking the 1980 census. High on the list was mapping. Every person counted in a census is pinpointed at a particular location, making accurate geography important. For the 1980 census, it took about 200 local agencies, 1,600 employees from the Census Bureau, and a private contractor four years to draw 32,000 maps. They plotted boundaries, added streets and features with press-on type, and assigned block numbers by hand. Many of the resulting hand-made maps were hard for enumerators to read.

From the analysis of 1980 mapping problems came the idea for TIGER.

"Let's do it," said Stan. And Robert Marx, a geographer at the Census Bureau, led the census team that joined forces with the U.S. Geological Survey to do it.

Matchett went on to other challenging assignments. After managing one-half million temporary census enumerators in 1990 on time and on budget, he is now modernizing the Census Bureau with CASIC, or computer assisted survey information collection. CASIC is increasing the efficiency of the Census Bureau's surveys and censuses with notebook computers, voice recognition, touch-tone data entry, and computer-assisted telephone interviewing. Census Bureau staff such as Matchett and Marx defy the stereotype of do-nothing bureaucrats. Marx has now been chosen to direct the 2000 census.

The Census Bureau also borrows and adapts many of the technologies it uses. While the recording industry gave compact disks (CDs) their initial market, the Census Bureau put compact disks to practical use as a storage medium for masses of data. In doing so, the bureau democratized demographic data—making them available to anyone with a personal computer. After nearly two centuries of publishing its data in printed reports, and after several decades of producing them on computer tapes, the Census Bureau began putting its economic census data on CDs in 1987. One CD can contain all of the economic censuses, or the 1990 census population data for several medium-sized states, or the census population data for half of California.

All these technologies were in place for the 1990 census, plus other advances such as bar-coded mailing envelopes, high-speed microfilming, and a management information system that let the bureau's managers know the status of each of the 100 million-plus census questionnaires.

The Low-Tech Census

For all the high-tech advances and computer wizardry, there was plenty of low-tech in the 1990 census too. As I stood that day on the Jeffersonville loading dock, the operation looked a lot like what must have gone on when the Quartermaster Corps of the Grand Army of the Republic was there, except that the wagons of yesterday were now moving vans with diesel engines.

Binghamton and Elmira, New York, were the destinations for the vans being loaded as I watched. More moving vans waited behind them for their turn at the dock. Binghamton and Elmira were two of the 496 temporary district offices—9 in Puerto Rico and 487 in the 50 states—that would direct local operations and follow-up interviews with residents who did not mail back their census questionnaires. It took one van load to equip each census district office for start-up.

The Census Bureau distributed to the 496 offices some 68,000 cardboard desks, 25,000 cardboard tables, 16,000 miles of microfilm, 250,000 dozen pencils (1,200 miles of them if laid end to end, which we did not do) and 1.8 million packages of paper clips. The boxes of paper clips filled six tractor trailer trucks when they arrived at Jeffersonville.

"I hope they were made in the U.S.A.," quipped one of my colleagues in the International Trade Administration when I told the senior staff at the Commerce Department about the paper clips. To my relief, the paper clips were manufactured by an organization in Texas that employs the handicapped.

The cardboard desks and tables are a census original, used for the last several enumerations. Designed jointly by the Census Bureau and a cardboard box company across the river from Jeffersonville in Louisville, Kentucky, each desk has a kneehole and an open shelf for paper but no drawers. To make them seem like real desks, the cardboard is printed with an oak grain. Not fancy, but the price was right—just $13 each. The specs called for each desk to be strong enough to hold a computer terminal for two years. There were no requirements for durability beyond 1992. The Census Bureau intended to recycle the desks when the district offices closed, but I'm told that some from the 1970 and 1980 censuses still lurk in basement playrooms.

Equipping nearly 500 offices requires a certain uniformity. Each 1990 office was supplied with the same equipment, including cardboard room dividers for turning large rented rooms into separate work areas. In all, the Census Bureau had to rent the equivalent in floor space of 2.2 Empire State buildings. The district office manager in San Juan, Puerto Rico, admonished me that it was unnecessary to ship coat racks to a place where employees don't wear coats. He then complained that the cardboard room dividers were curling up in the humidity. Later he discovered that the coat racks were useful after all—he used them to reinforce the sagging cardboard room dividers.

Launching an Army

The U.S. population may be considerably smaller than China's, but reaching over 100 million households is still a massive operation. To count America's population in 1990, we launched the largest army the U.S. government has ever put into the field outside of war—over half a million temporary employees on top of our permanent staff of 9,000. About 2,000 of the bureau's permanent employees worked on the census, while the rest kept the Census Bureau's other ongoing surveys on track. Over the next year, it sometimes felt like we were at war—at least in the offices of mayors, the front pages of newspapers, on the nightly news, and at hearings in the committee rooms of Congress.

A major challenge of 1990 turned out to be how to hire the many temporary workers we needed in a near-full-employment economy. The jobless rate hovered between 5.0 and 5.4 percent during the months surrounding the census.

The 1990 census was the first in modern times without a large pool of housewives to sign up as temporary workers. There was only a puddle of housewives in 1990, and by 2000 even this puddle will dry up, since virtually all employable women will be working. Because we needed all the help we could get, the Department of Health and Human Services allowed states to waive census wages in determining eligibility for Aid to Families with Dependent Children. We were allowed to hire welfare recipients to work for us, and the money we paid them did not count in the calculation of their welfare benefits. AFDC mothers proved to be good workers when offered jobs in their own neighborhood that didn't take away their benefits. Likewise, the Department of Housing and Urban Development determined that the pay from temporary census jobs would not count in calculating eligibility for public housing. Congress passed a bill allowing retired federal and military employees to take census jobs without losing pension benefits. About one in ten temporary employees was a senior citizen, some the alumni of census taking as far back as 1960.

"What were you doing before you took this job?" I asked hundreds of temporary employees as I crisscrossed the country promoting the census. A few were welfare recipients who wanted to earn extra money. Some were recent retirees who found life at home a bore. Others were people considering a job change who needed a few months of temporary employment to examine their options.

The half-million temporary workers delivered questionnaires to about 10 million households that did not have mailable addresses. They paid personal visits to the millions of households with mailable addresses who did not return their mailed questionnaires. They combed and recombed the hardest-to-enumerate neighborhoods of the United States in an attempt to make the undercount as small as possible.

The 1990 census may well be the last with so many troops. What the Census Bureau learned from the 1990 census is that it cannot keep improving the accuracy of the census simply by throwing more troops into the fray. It's the low-tech aspects of the census that the bureau is trying to streamline for 2000. The bureau tested a variety of ways to transfer work from the foot soldiers to the statisticians with the 1995 test census. But whether the politicians and the public will let the bureau become more efficient is another question.

References

1. Carling, Jan, personal meeting with Barbara Everitt Bryant, Stockholm, March 7, 1994.

2. Noble, Kenneth (1991). "Census in Nigeria Halts Normal Life," *The New York Times*, November 29, 1991, p. A7.

3. Noble, Kenneth (1992). "After Nigeria's Census, Skeptic Count is High," *The New York Times*, June 4, 1992, p. A13.

4. Cohen, Roger (1994). "Macedonia Census Just Inflames the Disputes, *The New York Times*, July 17, 1994, p. 6.

5. Information on China's 1990 census obtained in meetings between personnel of the State Statistical Bureau, Beijing, the Shanghai Municipal Statistical Bureau, Barbara Everitt Bryant, and four professional staff members of the Bureau of the Census, April 1991.

6. *100 Years of Data Processing: The Punchcard Century* (Washington, D.C.: Bureau of the Census, January 1991), pp. 5-6.

7. Information Age Exhibit, Museum of American History/ Smithsonian Institutions, 1991—.

8. *200 Years of Census Taking: 1790-1990* (Washington, D.C.: Bureau of the Census, November 1989), pp. 28-33.

9. Anderson, Margo J. (1988). *The American Census: A Social History* (New Haven: Yale University Press, 1988), p. 102.

10. Reid-Green, Kenneth S. (1989). "The History of Census Tabulation," *Scientific American*, February 1989, pp. 98-103.

11. *100 Years of Data Processing*, pp. 15-16.

12. *Ibid*, p. 6.

13. *Ibid*, pp. 7-8.

14. Williams, Michael R. (1985). *A History of Computing Technology* (Englewood Cliffs, NJ: Prentice Hall, 1985), pp. 360-365.

15. Burks, Arthur and Alice Burks (1988). *The First Electronic Computer: The Anastoff Story* (Ann Arbor: University of Michigan Press, 1988), and telephone interview with Arthur Burks, Ann Arbor, Michigan, by Barbara Everitt Bryant, January 16, 1994.

16. *TIGER: The Coast-to-Coast Digital Map Data Base*, (Washington, DC: U.S. Department of Commerce, Bureau of the Census, November 1989).

CHAPTER 6

Resisting the Count

"Oh, you're the census lady," said someone with a Yiddish accent. I felt a punch-line coming, because my inquisitor was none other than comedian Jackie Mason, whose one-man show was running on Broadway.

"I am the director of the 1990 census, yes," I responded with a smile. I was at the January 1990 Washington Press Club "Salute to Congress" banquet, which I attended in hopes of cultivating some of the several hundred influential journalists who were also there. As a former journalist, I knew that one key to the success of the census was media coverage and support.

As census director, I was prepared to go anywhere at any time to promote, defend, and conduct the census. This job would take me from the bureau's command center in Suitland, Maryland, to Capitol Hill, to editorial board rooms, to community centers, radio talk shows, New York City's Port Authority bus terminal, and on this night to the Grand Hyatt Hotel in downtown Washington.

And while it isn't in the director's job description, I played straight man (or woman) for Jackie Mason. Our conversation went something like this:

"Do I count?"

"Of course, you count, we try to count everyone."

"'Ya mean ya count Jews?"

"We are not allowed to ask about religion. But, we intend to count everybody."

"When ya coming to my house? I want to get my answers ready."

"Census Day is April 1. Look for your questionnaire in the mail."

My encounter with Jackie Mason was good preparation for subsequent interviews with reporters, whose questions sometimes seemed like they were written by Mason. I assume Mason answered and returned his questionnaire. Too many others didn't, either from apathy, unwarranted fear, or hostility to the government.

Despite today's technologies, taking a census, whether in 1790 or 1990, is a balancing act between the public's trust and cooperation and the government's promise of confidentiality and mutual benefits. If any of these elements fail, the whole endeavor is at risk.

The decline in public trust and cooperation alarms many government officials and special-interest groups, all of whom have their own ideas about how to take a census. Their involvement has aided promotional efforts at the community level and helped to improve census-taking techniques, but it also means plenty of armchair quarterbacking, meddling, and distractions.

Many segments of the public were willing to work hard to get their people counted. Representatives of Black, Hispanic, American Indian, and Asian constituencies, for example, overwhelmed the Census Bureau with their demands. They were strident, but they were also cooperative.

Responding to these demands, the Census Bureau ran an enormous outreach campaign to promote answering the 1990 census, particularly among the groups most likely to be undercounted. The two predominant messages in this outreach campaign were: (1) your answers are confidential—the bureau, by law, cannot share data with any federal, state, or local agency, or with your landlord, or even with your mother-in-law; and (2) political and economic benefits accrue to your community when you are counted.

"Answer the Census, It Counts for More Than You Think," was the slogan of the 1990 census. The Census Bureau placed 280 census awareness specialists, most of them recruited from groups most likely to be undercounted, at its 13 regional census centers. More than a year before Census Day, these specialists went to work with community groups to sell the census themes. They involved 56,000 state and community organizations in their effort. They helped establish 350 state and city Complete Count Committees to get the twin messages of confidentiality and importance out to the public.

New York City cooperated with census outreach and promotion, even though it had filed suit against the Census Bureau two years before. This lawsuit set the media agenda, which in turn determined the public relations environment in which we had to orchestrate the 1990 census. The 1988 lawsuit definitely wasn't the kickoff the bureau had planned for the 1990 census. It was more like a kick in the pants.

Convincing the Cynics

As part of the 1990 promotional effort, the bureau toyed with the idea of sponsoring a made-for-TV movie about the dramatic history of census taking, to air around Census Day. The idea never got beyond brainstorming and may have been doomed by memories of a 1980 television soap opera whose script included a census taker shot after knocking on someone's door. We didn't need that kind of PR, although it foreshadowed an actual shooting during the 1990 census.

Instead of going the TV route, the bureau enlisted pro athletes, community leaders, and Miss America 1990, Debbye

Turner, to vouch for the census and its importance. Leaving nothing to chance, we also enlisted the indirect assistance of the Almighty. On Sunday, April 1, 1990, Census Day, and the preceding weekend, clergy at some 369,000 houses of worship took to their pulpits to urge parishioners to cooperate with the census and be counted.

"If you want Washington to pay more attention to you, fill out and send back your census questionnaire," said the clergy. Admittedly, that line doesn't have the same majestic turn of phrase found in the gospels, and it certainly wasn't divinely inspired. Actually, it was inspired by the Census Promotion Office, which wrote a message about the census and sent it to clergy across the nation.

I crisscrossed America to talk up the census. As a result, I got sandbagged in San Francisco's "tenderloin district," flew into Detroit in the middle of a snowstorm wearing orchid leis, previewed what would happen to Queen Elizabeth two years later at a press conference, and spent the longest three minutes of my life on the stage of Harlem's famed Apollo Theater with singer Marian Anderson.

The Complete Count Committee of San Francisco scheduled a mid-February press conference with me, coordinated by the National Coalition for an Accurate Count of Asian-Pacific Americans. What better way to promote our mutual goals, I thought. I didn't become suspicious until I reached the conference site—a crumbling, unheated hotel in a part of the city known locally as the "tenderloin district." Around a horseshoe-shaped table sat representatives of all the local advocacy groups who believed their people would never be fully counted. Each group got a chance to speak before I did, with newspaper reporters and TV cameras surrounding us in the 55-degree temperature. I sat where the stake would be if they had been tossing horseshoes, and that morning horseshoes did indeed fly. I had one advantage: coming from a northern climate, my fingers and toes did not numb as fast as those of the locals who wanted to show me how difficult it would be to count people in that district.

Pacific Islanders threw a warmer welcome. Anxious to get a complete count of Pacific Islanders living in the 50 states, groups representing those who had moved to the continental U.S. from Guam, Samoa, and other islands loaded me with flower leis at a Friday night census kickoff in Carson City, south of Los Angeles. I was still wearing the leis as I boarded the 10:45 P.M. "red eye" flight to Detroit, where I was to meet Michigan Senator Carl Levin and his staff. I was still wearing the leis as I disembarked from the plane. They were a nice souvenir, but they looked silly as I stood in four inches of snow at Detroit's Metropolitan Airport.

And then it was back to Washington, D.C., where the National Association of Religious Broadcasters was meeting. A big turnout was expected because President Bush was the keynote speaker. The Census Promotion Office squeezed me into the program for a five-minute pep talk, sandwiched between a hymn and the President.

When I reached the podium, I found myself face-to-face with the same problem that would confront Queen Elizabeth during her 1992 White House visit—the podium was topped with dozens of two-foot-tall microphones adjusted for a six-foot, three-inch man. I have about a four-inch height advantage over Her Majesty, and standing on tiptoes gave me an additional two inches. Try doing that for five minutes!

In Black neighborhoods, the poster promoting the census, designed by the Census Bureau's Promotion Office, bore the likeness of famous contralto Marian Anderson. The slogan on it was "lift every voice—stand up and be counted." At age 90, Miss

Anderson agreed to unveil the poster at Harlem's legendary Apollo Theater. She arrived in a wheelchair, attended by her nurse and two nieces.

The time came, and I introduced her to the audience. Dead silence. The audience held its collective breath. We waited. One minute of silence is long on center stage. Three minutes is an eternity.

"We pushed this wonderful, elderly woman too far," I thought. "We shouldn't have asked." I decided to wait another minute, then thank her for letting us use her likeness on the poster. I was about to do just that when, suddenly, her resonant voice filled the theater, electrifying the audience with her message of the importance of knowing who you are. We listened in rapt attention.

Targeting the Public

Watching a government bureaucracy try to do target marketing is like watching eight-year-old children at a summer camp on their first day at the rifle range. They may have the equipment, but they aren't sure where to point it.

The Census Promotion Office did many things right, but it went overboard in planning for 144 different promotional products—each of which was intended for a different audience. By January 1990, I realized that the Census Promotion Office had double the number of products it could produce and distribute effectively.

One of the promotional tools ready by mid-January was advertising—TV and radio spots developed by the Ad Council. For the first time, the Ad Council had chosen minority-owned ad agencies, The Mingo Group (Black), Castor Spanish GS&B (Hispanic), and Muse Cordero Chen (Asian), as well as the national ad agency Ogilvy and Mather to produce spots. The ads were creative and well targeted, but they were not linked with each other. The public-service spots on Black radio, for example, did not use the same slogan to promote the census as the general audience public-service spots on network TV. Spanish-language spots targeted to Mexican Americans, Puerto Ricans, and Cubans had design and copy themes unlike any others.

The Ad Council spots were ready by the deadline for media launch, but many other products were behind schedule. Hispanic organizations had been promised Spanish-language posters for their neighborhoods; Asians were waiting for brochures in a variety of Asian languages. Pencils, coffee mugs, plastic bags, and other novelties were still in production as the calendar relentlessly advanced into 1990.

So the census awareness specialists in the district offices did what people with a mission do. They began to produce promotional materials using their computer terminals and copying machines. These materials included as many designs as there were enthusiastic workers. Many did not use the slogan "Answer the census—it counts for more than you think," or the logo developed by the Ad Council.

"What's ready? What's almost ready? What must we cut and dump?" I asked my staff. "And how fast can we get materials out where they will do some good?"

Getting things out is something the Census Bureau knows how to do well. After all, the regional census offices complete about 150,000 survey interviews every month of the year, year in and year out. The bureau does have a network. Unfortunately, the network is designed for uniformity. It is not set up for target marketing.

With time running out, we had to send all 487 district offices in the 50 states the same shipments of promotional products. (Puerto Rico had a separate campaign well coordinated by the volunteer Ad Council agency, West Indes Grey.) We hoped offices in Mississippi or Indiana would just ignore the "Alaska Natives Be Counted" posters.

The trouble was that everybody loved the Alaska poster, created by artist Denise Wallace of the Institute of American Indian Arts (IAIA) in Santa Fe. I saw those posters everywhere, from Long Island to San Diego. Now, long after the 1990 census, they are collectors' items. One hangs on the wall of my office in the School of Business Administration at the University of Michigan.

I flinched upon entering an administrative building on the Tulalip Indian reservation north of Seattle. The entry hall looked like an art gallery of census posters. There was Marian Anderson saying "Stand Up for Who You Are." There was "*¡Esta Es La Nuestra! Participe En El Censo!*" There was the "Alaska Natives Be Counted" poster. The posters designed by other IAIA artists conveying the importance of the census to Indian tribes were there as well—but they were lost amid the art show.

Whatever the misfires in targeting, the combined efforts of the Census Promotion Office and media coverage—both positive and negative—achieved 97 percent awareness of the census among the U.S. public. [1] But awareness did not always translate into cooperation.

Beating the Thaw

While the official Census Day was April 1, 1990, in Alaska counting got underway in February. The 300-plus Alaska Native Villages are mostly fishing enclaves. Enumerators flew out in February with bush pilots, one to a village. The work started this early because once the ice breaks up, which can happen by April 1, floods often shut down village airstrips. After the thaw, many village residents leave on fishing expeditions.

Jeannette Cole packed her down boots and a sleeping bag rated to 40 degrees below zero. She slept in the tribal council building at night while she counted the approximately 140 households in Kwethluk, a village of Yupik Eskimos. In a liaison effort orchestrated by the Census Bureau, the village council chief had appointed two villagers to assist Cole, who was a stranger, in getting access to villagers.[2] Meanwhile, other enumerators were snowmobiling into remote areas, using frozen rivers as roads.

Street and Shelter Night

March 20, 1990: It was the eve of Street and Shelter Night, or S-Night as it is called. It was a pioneer event, the first big-time effort to count the homeless population in shelters and on the streets.

Mitch Snyder, the controversial advocate for the homeless, who died in 1993, started my day by dumping truckloads of sand on the street in front of the Commerce Department and in the driveway of the home of commerce secretary Robert A. Mosbacher. This made it hard for me to convince Mosbacher—my boss—that I had everything under control. Embedded in each pile of sand was a homemade sign that read, "Counting the homeless is like counting grains of sand."

Snyder was staging this protest and threatening to bar that night's census takers from entering the shelter he ran in Washington, D.C. He was urging other shelter providers to do the same to protest what he said would be a certain undercount of the homeless population.

He claimed that there were at least 3 million homeless Americans. He had reiterated this assertion since the early 1980s, and had testified on the subject before a Congressional committee in 1984. Asked to explain his number, he said it was meaningless. "We have tried to satisfy your gnawing curiosity for a number because we are Americans with Western little minds that have to quantify everything in sight, whether we can or not," Snyder responded.[3] Snyder was protesting the census count of the homeless because he knew the bureau would count far less than the politically potent, but fictional, 3 million. No previous estimate of the homeless based on surveys had ever come close to that number.

There is no doubt that the homeless population grew during the 1980s. Every mayor in every city across the country is now sensitive to this population. They want their homeless counted. Since the census counts people by counting the residents of housing units, the Census Bureau knows it must use different methods to count those without fixed addresses. That's what S-Night was all about.

We were prepared for Snyder's resistance. My third-in-command, Pete Bounpane, and a team led by bureau employee Charles Moore, would stand their ground that night, counting residents as they entered and exited shelters if they were refused admittance. I learned later that Snyder tore up census forms in front of TV cameras, arguing that the census would miss many more homeless than it would count, thereby understating the problem. Undoubtedly, the census would miss some of the homeless. But how could mayors and policy makers ever hope to resolve the problem if we didn't start somewhere? Made-up numbers such as Snyder's 3 million are worthless to policy makers and to advocates who truly want to help the homeless.

Mitch Snyder's needless confrontation with the Census Bureau is but one example of Americans' schizophrenia about data. On the one hand, we demand total accuracy, pointing to the high stakes riding on census numbers. On the other hand, too many Americans either don't want to be counted or have their own agendas, pursuing narrow self-interests. "Count me if you can, but don't count on me," is the all-too-common attitude. On S-Night, bureau personnel and local enumerators fanned out across the nation. I spent S-Night driving around to shelters in Manhattan and the Bronx, to the Port Authority Terminal, and walking the streets of New York City wearing Reeboks, slacks, and jacket in a drizzling rain.

This was a night for theater, but not of the kind found on Broadway. To show our good faith effort to count the homeless, the Census Bureau's entire executive staff joined in to monitor S-Night. Deputy Director Kincannon ended up stuck in a truck in the Salt River Valley outside Phoenix at 2:00 A.M. The chief of congressional affairs, A. Mark Neuman, was photographed by the *Chicago Tribune* with flashlight in hand as he monitored counting on underground Wacker Drive.

In total, there were 23,000 census takers at work that night, including several hundred recruited from among the homeless and others who provide services for them. They know best where homeless people will bed down. In pairs, enumerators visited places that most people would never go, even in daylight. They walked into parks, peered into caves, tramped along river beds, scoured the bowels of bus and train stations, looked into the doorways of abandoned buildings, and searched under highway overpasses and bridges. I refused to ask anyone on my staff or among the temporary workers to go places I would not. And that's why I, too, was on the streets this night.

I would take the stage at press conferences both that night and the next morning to explain S-Night to the public. I would speak at many more press conferences before the census was over. I would also appear at Congressional hearings, half of which—all the controversial ones—would be covered by C-Span. Taking a census is more theater than I realized before I took the job of directing it.

Bright Lights, Big City, Too Many Reporters

The bright lights of theater marquees, garish souvenir shops, and video arcades glimmered two blocks to the east on Broadway. A block west loomed the green, art deco tower of the old McGraw-Hill building, where I began my career 43 years ago. Back then, I was a new physics graduate from Cornell with ambitions to be a science writer.

"In a long career, I have come exactly one block, but traveled far," I quipped to Sheila Grimm, New York's regional director of the Census Bureau, as we began our rounds.

S-Night has a little bit of everything that gets drilled into a student of Journalism 101—human interest, pathos, and controversy. Feature writers and reporters were hungry for the story.

That's why the Census Promotion Office and I orchestrated a media plan for S-Night that included press conferences in 50 cities a few hours before we began the count. Of course, the identities of those without an address are as confidential as the identities of those with addresses. Enumerators would be available for interviews before and after, but not during, the S-Night count. We warned reporters not to try to photograph, identify, or interview those being counted. We explained that enumerators have sworn an oath to uphold the confidentiality of individuals, with severe penalties for breaking it.

"And now, good-bye," I said at the New York City press conference. "Please don't follow as we count."

New York City was fully cooperative with us, as were most cities. David Dinkins, Koch's successor both as mayor of New York and as plaintiff on its lawsuit against us, wanted the homeless of his city counted. He gave the bureau a list of every city shelter. New York City had a carrot and stick approach to the 1990 census—cooperate and sue.

At a 400-bed men's shelter in the Bronx, shelter workers set up tables for census takers. City buses delivered homeless men to the shelter. There were also walk-ins. Shelter workers directed the men past the tables. A reporter who tried to enter in search of a story was politely but firmly told to leave by the shelter director. The director was determined to maintain the privacy and dignity of the homeless.

Elsewhere, enumerators had to run an obstacle course in front of network news cameras and lights reminiscent of the nighttime landing of U.S. Marines in Somalia a few years later. Census takers repeatedly stopped prying cameras from photographing them at work.

I monitored census takers in New York's Port Authority Terminal, a cavernous bus station that encompasses two multi-floor buildings. Underneath the buildings is a maze of subway access tunnels. It is a difficult place to do anything systematically, from catching a bus to reaching a subway and, especially, counting the homeless who sleep and loiter inside. When Sheila Grimm and I got there, enumerators—and the media—had been working for some time. The first thing we saw were TV film crews from all the major networks running around looking for the homeless on an upper level. But at the sight of census enumerators and cameras, the homeless sunk into the subway tunnels. Meanwhile, enumerators—following instructions—broke off interviews with any individual if a camera came into sight.

In an office in the early morning hours, we reviewed the Port Authority Terminal count to decide if we needed to redo it another night. The count was as large as anticipated by our pre-canvassing on prior nights. It was as good as possible in a place configured like the Port Authority Terminal.

Grand Central Terminal, Manhattan's majestic train station, was easier. Enumerators ringed its perimeter, then moved inward counting everyone in their path until they met in the center.

I phoned in to the hotline we set up at Census Bureau headquarters to handle emergencies, as I had been doing periodically all night. This time the news was not good. Two enumerators had been shot at from an abandoned Brooklyn building. The enumerators phoned 911 and were told to come to police headquarters to report the incident. Instead, they moved on to cover the rest of their assigned territory. The night was too short to deal with the local bureaucracy. An enumerator in Florida was robbed of her watch, jewelry, and cash, but was otherwise unharmed. We warned enumerators not to carry valuables.

Across the country we found some unexpected allies— prostitutes. (The enumerators were not supposed to count those out at night working for pay, whether police officers or others). Our new allies pointed out locations where the homeless sleep. Census takers counted the sleepers, and estimated their sex, age, and race if they could.

The Bureau repeatedly explained: S-Night is a count only of those in shelters or those visible on the streets. It is not a definitive count of the homeless. Nevertheless, the media insisted on reporting the historical undertaking as "the homeless census." From then on, they focused on how many homeless the Census Bureau missed. Advocates for the homeless fed the media with material.

While it would be months before the S-Night tally was analyzed and published, census takers on the night of March 20, 1990, counted 179,000 persons in over 12,000 shelters, and an additional 50,000 on streets and in abandoned buildings. It was the most comprehensive and complete count of persons in shelters ever made on a single night in the nation. None of us can vouch for the comprehensiveness of the street count. There are undoubtedly more homeless people—those who remain concealed in tunnels between subway stations, in abandoned cars, and other isolated places. People on the street are a moving target. While we know there are more than we counted, it is also clear that there are far less than 3 million. In fact, there are fewer than 1 million homeless in shelters or on the streets on a given night. The figures from S-Night, once released, were promptly and loudly dismissed by homeless advocates as grossly understating the homeless population.

Today the homeless advocates have a new and even larger figure—7 million homeless at some point in the 1980s. This number makes the late Mitch Snyder appear conservative. The new figure was released with fanfare—but without research or documentation—on February 16, 1994, in a draft of the Clinton Administration's to-be-revised plan to end homelessness. I wish them well, but I don't think they can substantiate their figures. [4]

In other phases of the 1990 census, we counted additional people who might be considered "homeless." There were 52,000 people in drug- and alcohol-rehab group homes. There were 12,000 in women's shelters. There were many people in campgrounds, some of whom were on vacation. We also found families doubled up in apartments and single-family homes. Some may have been living that way voluntarily, others because of a lack of housing. How many of these people should be considered homeless? There is no universal definition of the homeless except "those who live in shelters or on the streets."

The bureau accomplished what it set out to do. It added one-quarter of a million people to the count who would have been missed without S-Night. We also protected the confidentiality of those counted that night. No name was ever revealed as a result of the S-Night count.

The Census Bureau did not provide a count of all the homeless in the United States, however, and we never said we would. For that, we got sued. More than two years after the census, on October 8, 1992, the National Law Center on Homelessness and Poverty, the United States Conference of Mayors, the City of Baltimore, the City and County of San Francisco, and 26 organizations that provide services for the homeless filed suit against the bureau. Thus the 1990 census was bracketed by lawsuits two years before and two years after the census.

In the best of all possible worlds, it may be beneficial for the public to take the Census Bureau to court repeatedly, forcing it to prove the accuracy and fairness of its census-taking techniques over and over again. But this is not the best of all possible worlds. It is a world fueled by finite amounts of money and power. It is a zero-sum game in which special-interest groups try to boost census results in their favor, and each is willing to go to court to do so. In the real world, the census and the Census Bureau are under siege. Special-interest groups have made a circus out of the census, with Congress as the ringmaster.

References

1. Fay, Robert, Nancy Bates and Jeffrey Moore (1991). "Lower Mail Response in the 1990 Census, A Preliminary Interpretation," *Proceedings, 1991 Annual Research Conference* (Washington, D.C.: Bureau of the Census, 1991), p. 9.

2. Bernton, Hal (1990). "Cold Hard Facts Are Harder and Colder to Gather in Eskimo Villages," *The Washington Post,* March 3, 1990, p. A3.

3. Price, Joyce (1991). "Bean counts of U.S. homeless range from 230,000 to 3 million," *The Washington Times,* April 18, 1991, p. A5.

4. DeParle, Jason (1994). "Report to Clinton Sees Vast Extent of Homelessness," *The New York Times,* February 17, 1994, p. A1.

CHAPTER 7

Circus of Politics

Congress, which monitors and holds the purse strings to the Census Bureau, stands atop Capitol Hill, a place of majestic beauty, great power, high drama, and occasional farce.

The Census Bureau is just eight miles and a world away in suburban Maryland, camouflaged in a sprawling complex of drab, three-story, tan brick buildings that shout "1940s government issue."

The 20-minute drive to Capitol Hill from the bureau quickly becomes a regular commute, no matter who happens to be the occupant of the census director's office in Federal Office Building 3. Occasionally, the commute is a courtesy call to the office of a powerful senator or representative. Most often the journey, made with entourage, is to 311 CHOB—the third-floor hearing room of Cannon House Office Building, assigned to the Subcommittee on Census, Statistics, and Postal Personnel. For years, the subcommittee held hearings on the bureau until it was eliminated and its responsibilities reassigned in 1995.

In my initial forays to the Hill, I was an unknown commodity, an outsider in an insiders' town. This had both advantages and disadvantages. I blew in from outside the beltway. More than just the ring of interstate highways that bound and define the Washington metropolitan area, the beltway separates the insiders—those who know how to survive in government—from the outsiders. I was from way outside, and unlike most presidential appointees, I had never served in government before. But I'm a quick learner and tougher than my brightly colored suits might suggest.

I also became director of the Census Bureau without the customary Senate confirmation hearing. At such hearings, Senators make nominees jump through hoops and then judge them on their nimbleness, point of view, and ability to withstand probing questions. Through the confirmation process, Congress and the interested public get to take the measure of the person with whom they will be dealing. But I had cleared this obstacle course by going around it, as it were, since President Bush used the arcane power of a recess appointment to install me in the director's chair while the Congress was on its 1989 Christmas recess.

For this reason, and because I was already running the $2.6 billion decennial census that would reapportion the House of Representatives, I was a mystery woman for the assorted House and Senate committees charged with census oversight—not on anybody's Rolodex.

As the publication *City and State* put it, "For the most part Ms. Bryant is an unknown in Washington. Those who have met her during the past few months say she is bright, accessible, nice—but untested. She never has been a public-sector employee, although she served on an advisory committee to the Census Bureau for six years." [1]

"She still has to be proven," said Jack Kaufman, a General Accounting Office assignment manager stationed at the Census Bureau. "Can she be a good manager on such a grand scale?"

Murdered by Questions

Appearances before Congress usually come one day after a "Murder Board." This is an ingenious exercise required by the Commerce Department when any of its senior staff are scheduled to testify before a Congressional committee. The Commerce brass figure that the way to reduce the stress of testifying before Congress and the TV news is to get thoroughly stressed out by your colleagues the day before. At the Murder Board's mock hearing, the colleagues who know the issues, as well as representatives of the General Counsel, and Legislative and Intergovernmental Affairs Offices, throw mean questions at you.

Three of my favorite colleagues made the sharpest rapier thrusts: Mark Plant, Under Secretary Darby's deputy; Harry Scarr, a career civil servant who was the top statistical person on the under secretary's staff (and now the deputy director of the Census Bureau, succeeding C. Louis Kincannon); and Lynn West, deputy general counsel—a disarmingly gentle-looking lawyer—took turns knifing me at Murder Boards. But once I figured out the answers to their questions, I could withstand anything members of Congress threw at me—well *practically* anything.

The Murder Board can prepare you for blazing hard balls, curve balls, and cheap shots. It cannot prepare you for the pitch that comes out of nowhere, however. That one came during my debut appearance before the House Appropriations Committee's Subcommittee on Commerce, State, and Justice. I was there in early 1990 to defend the Census Bureau budget proposed for fiscal 1991.

Michael Darby, under secretary of economic affairs, was on first, giving an overview of the economic statistics budget for the Commerce Department. He then introduced me to answer questions about the bureau's budget. I had done my homework, memorizing every detail of how we planned to spend the money we were requesting. I knew everything about the 1991 budget. The trouble was, I didn't know about 1972.

Representative Neal Smith, the subcommittee chairman from the farm state of Iowa, asked the first question. "Have you done anything about correcting the serious undercount of cattle in the 1972 agricultural census?" he demanded.

"Cattle? 1972?" I was flustered. "I'm afraid 1972 was before my time," I answered, turning desperately to my deputy Kincannon. The year 1972 was before his time as deputy director. At a Congressional hearing, expect the unexpected! The episode also reinforced one of the survival rules I'd been taught by Congressional affairs personnel at the Census Bureau and at the Commerce Department: when in doubt, don't guess. Instead, say "I don't have that information at hand, but I will get back to you in writing." Then do so. I did. Ask me anything about the count of cattle in 1972.

Most Congressional oversight of the census comes from the House side. After all, the count and its resulting reapportionment and redistricting are relevant to the jobs of every member. In the House, the key committee until 1995 was the Subcommittee on Census, Statistics, and Postal Personnel of the Committee on Post Office and Civil Service. On the Senate side, the watch dog of the Census Bureau is the Subcommittee on Government Regulation and Information of the Committee on Governmental Affairs.

During my tenure, the chairman of the House Subcommittee on the Census was Thomas C. Sawyer (D) of Akron, Ohio. Its ranking minority member was Thomas Ridge (R) of Erie, Pennsylvania. The Chairman of the Senate Subcommittee was Herbert Kohl (D) of Wisconsin. In the 1994 election, Ridge would become the Governor of Pennsylvania. Despite the Republican landslide, Sawyer and Kohl would be reelected.

Sawyer looks like the Tom Sawyer his name suggests, though I've learned he won't whitewash anything—whether picket fences, Census Bureau mistakes, or statistics. However, he will commend the Census Bureau when he thinks we've done something well.

Tom Ridge is a personable Vietnam veteran I was prepared not to like. While I was a bureau consultant not yet in office, he and Senator Richard C. Shelby of Alabama (a Democrat who would later switch to Republican) tried to pass an amendment to the 1990 budget to prohibit the Census Bureau from counting illegal aliens for apportionment purposes.

I was opposed to this for several reasons, as were those involved with the decennial census at the bureau. First, it would interfere with the bureau's outreach efforts to get Hispanics—whether citizens, legal immigrants, or undocumented immigrants—counted. Second, operationally there is no good way of asking the question, "Are you an illegal?" Third, the questionnaires, which took six months to print, were already rolling off the presses. Finally, and most important of all, the Constitution says we must enumerate all those *resident* in the United States, with no qualifications as to their status. Fortunately, the amendment was defeated.

When I finally met Ridge, to my surprise I liked him. He hit the issue head on: "I made an attempt, I lost, now the important thing is do the best job we can of counting everyone in the census. You have my support for that." I found Ridge and Sawyer an interesting pair. Although from opposite sides of the political aisle and not always in agreement, they had clearly decided to run the subcommittee cooperatively.

Lights, Camera, Action

The presence or absence of the blinding lights of C-SPAN was a good indication of whether or not a Congressional hearing would be hot—politically hot that is.

Hearings begin at 10:00 A.M. sharp. Sawyer and Ridge always invited what was meant to be a balanced panel of witnesses, but to me often seemed disproportionately made up of census critics. Witnesses included myself, representatives of the General Accounting Office (GAO), and three to five others. The protocol order was: Senators, Representatives, census director, GAO (immediately before or after me), other witnesses. Since members of Congress were witnesses only occasionally, the usual order was me, the GAO, and unhappy mayors.

At times, and usually when the hearing was expected to be controversial, there were phantom witnesses whose written and highly quotable testimony was dropped on the press table by an aide with the testifier nowhere in sight. Sometimes stories were written by reporters who weren't there, or who didn't stick around for the entire hearing. Instead, they wrote their dispatches from the testimony on the press table or from handouts sent directly to their offices by messenger.

Aides felt no qualms about darting into the high-ceilinged hearing room in the middle of a hearing to drop 50 or so copies of someone's testimony on the press table, which was right behind the witness table. The smack of a stack of testimony hitting the press table was like a shot from a starter's pistol. It sent most of the onlookers in the room—people from the Census Bureau and other agencies, Congressional staffers, the representatives of assorted interest groups, and tourists—all scurrying from their chairs to get their copy. Like locusts dining on a bumper crop of summer wheat in Kansas, the observers stripped the press table bare of testimony. Amid this activity, I had to keep my cool and continue on with my testimony.

Unlike phantom witnesses, I always appeared to testify. In my appearance before Sawyer's subcommittee on March 27, 1990, I reported confidently that the census was underway with all preparations completed, on time and on budget. I did point out, however, that the bureau's $2.6 billion ten-year budget approved by Congress had been eroded by about $100 million by unanticipated mandated expenses. Salary increases and a one-penny-per-mile additional allowance for travel using personal vehicles (pennies add up with half a million temporary enumerators heading into the field) took their toll. But we had saved money in the printing of questionnaires. We could manage with what we had. The statements of the Congressmen on the Subcommittee who questioned me, Rep. Mervyn Dymally of California and Rep. Michael R. McNulty of New York, kept up the litany predicting an undercount, a litany that had begun with the New York City lawsuit in 1988.

By April 23 I knew the meaning of the word "crisis." That was the date when we had to print the addresses of all the housing units that had not responded to the census, extracting them from our management information system. Each district office gave its enumerators the local address list of non-responding housing units. The enumerators then visited each one. As we processed returns, we discovered that the return rate was only 63 percent. In 1970, 78 percent of housing units returned their mailed questionnaires. In 1980, 75 percent returned them. In 1990, the Census Bureau had budgeted for a return rate of 70 percent. A drop of 7 percentage points may not sound that critical, but this meant we needed to make over 6 million additional house calls.

Something had not worked. At that time we did not know why, though we would later learn through research that there were many reasons--but no single, major reason. What we did know then was that response was 12 percentage points lower than it had been ten years earlier and 7 percentage points lower than we had funds or staff to cover. Our crisis was one of money, people, and time—and we had to work on all three at once. Getting money was the priority for me as director.

On April 19, four days before the cut-off date for printing the address lists and with response at only 62 percent, I entered

Room 311 of the Cannon Office Building again.[2] This time my message was considerably different from the "on time, on budget" report of three weeks earlier.

"Mr. Chairman," I alerted Sawyer, Ridge, and a lineup of C-SPAN, CNN, NBC, ABC, and CBS cameras, as well as reporters from all the national dailies and the Associated Press at a table behind me. "We are going to need on the order of $110 million and we will need it fast. We're sending the census takers out to follow up on non-respondents next week to keep on schedule, but we'll run out of money before we are finished. Besides, we've got to recruit more people to work on this."

My knowledge of the bureau's desperate need for additional funding gave me the boost I needed to calm my nerves and sound confidently in charge. Charlie Jones, the career civil servant executive in charge of the 1990 census, sat next to me to answer any questions if I needed extra facts. Both of us looked under control. Neither of us felt that way.

In one of those miracles that occasionally happen in Washington, Congress granted the funds. And in one of those financial deals that are also a given in Washington, the money came in two packages. About $70 million came from an amendment to the emergency appropriation bill for economic aid to Panama and Nicaragua then moving through Congress. The rest came from releasing money we were required to set aside in the census budget as unemployment compensation for temporary employees—a release that was to cause me political and budget problems later, but that I was willing to worry about some other time.

This was the most critical of the 25 Congressional hearings at which I testified during my term. But it was not the most stressful. Congress did not blame the bureau for the crisis; it blamed the public.

Both Congressmen Sawyer and Ridge did their homework.

They knew and understood census operations. For the next three and one-half years, Sawyer and Ridge never let me off the hook, but I could not complain that they treated me or the Census Bureau unfairly, although many of the witnesses they invited to testify were harshly critical of the census. Clearly, Sawyer and Ridge helped save the 1990 census by supporting our need for funds in the crunch of a non-responding public.

The following month, May 21, 1990, the witnesses they invited for a hearing in the Federal Building in Manhattan included five Congressmen from New York City and New York state (Schumer and McNulty among them), the GAO, then me. I came on after six adversaries. I was followed by two temporary census enumerators having problems getting responses in New York City, representatives of two Hispanic groups who were certain we would undercount Hispanics, and an executive of the American Jewish Congress (though the census doesn't identify anyone by religion). Additionally, statements were submitted by Mayor Dinkins of New York City, the speaker of the New York State Assembly, the president of the Borough of Brooklyn, a representative of the Borough of Queens, and the president of the New York City League of Women Voters. Boy, did I feel like I was sandwiched on both sides!

The Three-Ring Circus

In appearing before any Congressional committee, the marching orders handed down to me from the Commerce Department were to arrive just prior to the hearing's 10:00 A.M. gavel, wait my turn to testify, testify, and then return to the Census Bureau in Suitland, Maryland. Other government officials follow the same drill. The reasons are both practical and strategic: there's work to do back at the office, and by leaving promptly you take yourself out of the range of reporters, except for quick questions on the way down the marble hallway.

Other witnesses—particularly critics eager to be quoted—tend to tarry, loitering just beyond the oaken doors to field reporters' questions. Consequently, each time someone completes his or her testimony and departs, so too do the attending press corps. Outside the doors, they pepper departing witnesses with questions in hopes of getting fresh quotes, even an exclusive.

Press coverage works the same way on the road as on Capitol Hill. While I was giving my testimony before Sawyer's subcommittee at that May 21 hearing in New York City, Rep. Charles Schumer was expounding in the hallway on the failings of the 1990 census and the need for adjustment.

My daughter, a Long Island textile designer who teaches at the Parsons School of Design in Manhattan, had hopped the subway from school to root for her mother. On her way out of the hearing room, she approached a small circle of reporters listening intently to Mr. Schumer, who was upbraiding the bureau and me for bungling a census that had barely gotten under way. Undoubtedly, he was replaying his favorite analogy—that we were trying to count New York City like Salina, Kansas.

The reporters scribbled copious notes, getting colorful comment from the Brooklyn representative. But all my daughter knew or cared about was that someone was criticizing her mother.

"Mom, you should have heard the things he was saying about you," she sputtered angrily when I saw her later. "And then he greets you so warmly!" In defense of her mother, my daughter was ready to pop him.

I chuckled at her reaction. I was becoming an insider. I was beginning to accept and even expect criticism from some members of Congress and special interest groups, even if I didn't like it or agree with it. Actually, in an adversarial way, I was beginning to enjoy sparring with Schumer.

Not even needing the platform of a hearing, Schumer and other legislators were firing off a steady barrage of press releases to news organizations, keeping reporters busy and the census on the front page. The constant, premature carping was part of a campaign to sway public perception and to pressure the bureau and the courts to adjust the census.

Two months before the census officially began, Schumer's office had issued a press release. It asserted: "Every bit of evidence available points to another massive undercount of New Yorkers; the question is not whether New York residents will be missed, but how many." Nearly simultaneously, on February 27, 1990, he wrote an op-ed piece for *The New York Times* entitled, "Shortchanged by the Census." [3]

Another memorable press release issued from his office proclaimed in capital letters: "SCHUMER REPORT DOCUMENTS CENSUS DISASTERS; HUNDREDS OF THOUSANDS OF NEW YORKERS HAVE NOT RECEIVED FORM IN THE MAIL; CITY FACES LOSS OF UP TO ONE BILLION DOLLARS." The release date was April 2, 1990—just one day after the official Census Day.

Three weeks later, the busy Rep. Schumer joined several prominent Democrats from Congress as well as Democratic National Committee chairman Ronald Brown (who would become secretary of commerce in the Clinton administration) at a press conference to pronounce the initial phase of the decennial census a flop.

"It's obvious that the first phase of the census process was a failure," Rep. Vic Fazio of California told assembled reporters. Referring to the undercount of minorities in past censuses and expecting a repeat in 1990, Fazio told *The New York Times*: "If the census is not working well, there are political spin-offs...We as Democrats can't stand by and let this travesty impact on the people who have the least influence." [4,5]

In their attempt at balanced coverage, reporters invariably led with the latest bad news, inserted a defending quote from a bureau official, then went back to more criticism. In her story on the Democrats' press conference, Felicity Barringer reported on page one of *The New York Times*:

> Dr. Bryant lashed out at critics of the 1990 census, saying they were only making things worse. "It doesn't help our role of trying to get everyone to cooperate when there are people out there saying, 'You're no good,'" Dr. Bryant said. "There are a lot of sour grapes before we've picked the grapes off the vine." [6]

My stress meter went into the red zone at that May hearing in New York. The General Accounting Office claimed the bureau's management information system records were causing problems, not producing data on follow-up interviews at households.

This was flat-out wrong! Because the GAO, the watchdog of Congress, is in the Rolodex of practically every reporter covering Washington, its reports become the ammunition of investigative reporters. That's what happened with this one. Reporters ran with the GAO's erroneous report. It wasn't until several weeks later that there was an admission from the GAO that its analysts had been examining data that were several weeks old. The GAO could not find house-call data because it was looking at computer printouts produced before enumerators started to make house calls. By the time of the hearing, we were producing daily reports with results from follow-up calls.

Most of the time, GAO testimony was accurate but pessimistic, always predicting dire consequences. I was raised to be an optimist. As my father used to say, "The pessimists may be right in the long run, but we optimists have more fun on the trip." As an optimist, I am psychologically unsuited to ever work for the General Accounting Office, although I respect the watchdog role it plays.

Heading Toward 2000

One of the last Congressional hearings at which I testified as census director was also the very first hearing on the 2000 census. The issue of privacy came up. Naturally, it came up in a discussion of how to cut the costs of census taking.

The hearing was being held by the Subcommittee on Government Information and Regulation, chaired by Senator Kohl. The date was June 26, 1992, and Kohl had invited me to testify (such "invitations" are virtually mandatory) about potential ways to reduce the cost of the next census.

"There is a growing fear that we cannot improve accuracy by pouring more money into the existing system," Kohl said. "So we need to think about alternatives." There were many things Senator Kohl and I did not agree on, but on the need for change in census-taking procedures we were in complete accord.

He had invited me to testify about the potential for using administrative lists—other government records—for improving the next census. Other government records, I responded, were not complete enough to replace the census. But "administrative records, if not usable for all purposes of a census, may have a potential for providing data on those who did not respond or identifying those the census missed." [7]

I then pointed out that "the Census Bureau's use of administrative records falls under the confidentiality protection of the law under which we operate, which, as you know, is Title 13 of the U.S. Code...And that same law that requires that we keep everything confidential also requires that we obtain and use administrative records to the greatest extent possible."

Until Senator Kohl's 1992 hearing, no Congressional hearing at which I testified had dealt specifically with confidentiality or the privacy issue. I had, however, often added a reminder of the confidentiality law that governs the census to my Congressional testimonies. Public awareness of the law needs constant reinforcement because few Americans realize they have this protection.

Following me as a witness at the hearing was Dr. Martin H. David, a professor of economics at the University of Wisconsin. "Some will object that linking administrative record systems to find an unduplicated count of people by address is an invasion of privacy," he said. But he continued, "I think 'one man, one vote' takes precedence over these concerns in a democratic society. People's protection under law and the Constitution does not mean they can elect not to be counted for apportionment." [8]

It was only minutes until we heard from one who objected. Janlori Goldman, director of the Privacy and Technology Project of the American Civil Liberties Union, testified after Professor David.

"...We have to strenuously object to the proposal before us to use administrative records on three grounds, one being the Privacy Act of 1974," she said. "The Privacy Act's main goal is to limit the disclosure of personal information from one agency at the federal government level to another agency." [9]

Her other reasons for opposition were that administrative records might be unreliable, and that using the records would betray the public trust. She conceded, however, that the Privacy Act made an exception for the Census Bureau when taking the census.

Despite the opposition of the ACLU and other privacy advocates, the Census Bureau almost certainly will use some records from federal, state, and local governments to improve the 2000 census. There is simply too much pressure to reduce both undercount and cost to avoid doing so. If the bureau does tap these records, privacy advocates will be unable to prevent it because of the provisions of Section 6 of Title 13. It's unlikely that privacy interests can get Congress to amend this law to exclude the bureau's use of outside data.

Having survived 25 Congressional hearings during my tenure as director, I find it far more enjoyable to watch hearings on C-SPAN in the family room of my Ann Arbor home than to be there live on the firing line. And while we don't personally keep in touch, I have kept up with Mr. Schumer via the nightly news. I admit that I've come to appreciate, even enjoy, the energetic legislator from Flatbush who keeps moving on to the most newsworthy issue of the day. He'll probably be around to parry with the director of the Census Bureau in 2000 as well. Of course, with remote control in hand, I now have the option of zapping him off my screen.

To be sure, Congress plays a vital role in census taking and the operations of the Census Bureau. Not only does it provide the bureau with funds, but its oversight can provide a valuable outside perspective when it is focused and constructive. Congressional hearings also offer an important window through which the public can see the inner workings of the bureau.

Sometimes, though, Congressional attention generates more heat than light. Legislators often provide more distractions than direction. The Census Bureau needs allies who understand the difficulties of census taking, who know what is possible and what is not. It needs allies who can put aside partisanship and parochial interests to provide the bureau with constructive criticism when needed and support when warranted. Unfortunately, the bureau's allies are few and far between.

References

1. Perlman, Ellen (1990). "Cities count on new director for an accurate 1990 census," *City and State*, February 12-25, 1990. pp. 1, 21.

2. 63 percent was the return rate when the bureau was budgeting and preparing lists for follow-up on non-respondents and seeking the supplemental appropriation from Congress. It had been 62 percent at the time of the Congressional hearing alerting the Subcommittee that there would be a need for additional funding. The rate climbed to 65 percent by April 23, 1990, when follow-up started, and to 66 percent in early May.

3. Schumer, Charles E. (1990). "Shortchanged by the Census," *The New York Times*, February 27, 1990, p. A23.

4. Barringer, Felicity (1990). "Democrats Say a Failed Census Needs a Change," *The New York Times*, April 20, 1990, p. A1.

5. Vobejda, Barbara (1990). "Finger-Pointing Begins Over Census," *The Washington Post*, April 20, 1990, p. A10.

6. Barringer, p. A1.

7. Transcript of hearing of Subcommittee on Government Information and Regulation, Committee on Governmental Affairs, June 26, 1992, p. 7.

8. *Ibid*, p. 16.

9. *Ibid*, p. 17.

CHAPTER 8

Why Response Is Down

The Census Bureau knows how many people do not respond to the census. Through research it estimates the number and characteristics of those who don't respond. The big question is why they don't.

Immediately after mail returns were in from the 1990 census, the bureau launched research to find out why many households did not return their questionnaires. I hoped there would be one major reason. I was even willing to discover that the bureau had made some big mistake. Instead, the reasons proved to be a bit of this and a bit of that. This means there is no easy fix for census 2000, when response rates are likely to drop even lower.

In every state, response rates in 1990 were lower than in 1980. Whatever the problem, it was pervasive. One theory was that the proliferation of junk mail had lowered response rates. But the junk mail theory washed out. In fact, research showed that those who receive the most direct mail belong to more organizations than the average person, are more likely to be registered to vote, and have higher rates of civic participation—including returning their census forms. "Being deluged with mail, requests for other surveys, and the like—were actually positively associated with census participation," [1,2] according to the National Opinion Research Center (NORC) of the University of Chicago.

NORC fielded a national survey for the Census Bureau to find out why people did not respond to the census. Dr. Richard Kulka and his colleagues at NORC discovered that 11 percent of the households that did not respond to the census claimed they had not received a census questionnaire or had not realized they had received one.[3] This was the single biggest reason for non-response.

While a smaller percentage of mailed questionnaires were returned unopened by the Postal Service in 1990 than in 1980, there were still some delivery problems. And many people just didn't seem to notice or recognize the arrival of their census questionnaire. To alleviate this problem in census 2000, the bureau plans to use a more accurate master address file. It will mail an advance letter alerting each household to look for its census questionnaire in the mail the following week. The bureau will also mail a reminder letter after sending the questionnaire, and finally it will mail a second questionnaire to those who still haven't responded. It tried out these procedures in the 1995 test census.

Another reason for non-response is the growing proportion of Americans who live with people to whom they are not related.[4,5] In such households, no one person is responsible for the household's paperwork. The census questionnaire may sit in the front hall for a while, then gets thrown away. In 2000, the questionnaire will be redesigned to accommodate non-traditional households, with separate blocks of questions for each individual to answer. Still, the form won't make it off the table in the front hall unless the advance and reminder letters get someone's attention.

Concerns about privacy and confidentiality also played a part in the non-response.[6] There is a segment of the population that is consciously opposed to the census. Though most Americans are not highly concerned about privacy and confidentiality, some are quite concerned.

There is "a sizable minority of citizens for whom these

concerns are indeed quite high, and persons with such concerns are in fact less likely than others to complete a census form and mail it back," report Kulka and his colleagues. NORC researchers found that "a general sense of alienation and lack of connectedness with society do indeed appear to inhibit participation in the census."[7] NORC research also revealed that those highly concerned about privacy and confidentiality were more likely than the average household to say they had not received a census questionnaire.

The NORC group created an index based on a series of questions that measure people's privacy concerns. They discovered that while only 14 percent of Americans feel their privacy is violated by the government when it takes the census, those 14 percent were 12 percentage points less likely to mail back their 1990 questionnaire than those who said the census did not violate their privacy.

Most Americans are concerned about "computers that store a lot of information about you." But this group returned its 1990 census forms at virtually the same rate as those who are not concerned about computers invading their privacy.[8]

Do you ever feel your privacy is being violated by:

(percent answering "yes")

Computers that store a lot of information about you	55%
Banks and credit companies when they ask about your finances	42
Neighbors who gossip about you and your family	29
The government when it collects tax returns	22
The people who ask questions on public opinion surveys	22
The government when it takes the census	14

SOURCE: *National Opinion Research Center, 1990*

Return rates varied greatly by demographic characteristics. Return rates were much lower among young adults than among older people: the response rate among people under age 30 was 28 percentage points below that of people aged 60 or older.[9] Blacks and Hispanics returned their forms at significantly lower rates than did non-Hispanic Whites. Yet the promotional evaluation survey showed awareness of the census was high among all groups: non-Hispanic Whites (99 percent), Blacks (89 percent) and Hispanics (96 percent).[10] Return rates rose with education and with income up to $75,000, then trailed off. Return rates were higher in the Midwest than on either coast.[11,12]

Loser of the Week

Press relations are like poor relations: They love you most when you fail. *Time* magazine made me its "loser of the week" in its April 23, 1990, issue: "Though it's not all her fault, the census director seems to have lost almost half of us," *Time* reported.[13]

Half was a bit of an overstatement. By the time we had to produce the address lists for follow-up house calls, the same day that the *Time* issue hit the newsstands, we did not know the whereabouts of 37 percent of census forms—although our management information system identified the addresses to which they had been sent. Census takers would discover that about 10 percent were vacant or seasonal housing units. The rest were households with real people in them, people who had not returned their forms and who the enumerators now had to track down.

The Census Bureau and the media have a symbiotic relationship. Census taking is highly dependent upon voluntary cooperation. Although the law requires people to answer the census, the fine is only $100 and is pretty much unenforceable. The bureau depends on the media to alert the public to the census and its benefits. Now the media were alerting the public to a "failed census," although census taking was still underway. Some of the headlines from April 1990 were brutal:

"'Bunch of junk': Census forms ignored"
—*USA Today*, April 13

"Slow Response to Census May Cost Millions Extra"
—*The Washington Post*, April 13

"Americans Find Many Excuses for Not Being Part of the Census"
—*The New York Times*, April 13

"Democrats Say a Failed Census Needs a Change"
—*The New York Times*, April 19

"Finger-pointing Begins Over Census: Politicians Blame Bureau for Citizenry's Poor Response"
—*The Washington Post*, April 20

"Apathy and Foul-Ups Foil the Census"
—*Newsweek*, April 30

Small wonder the April 19 Congressional hearing, at which I appealed for extra funds, and the May 21 hearing in New York City were so well covered by the press. Local politicians and special-interest groups thought the census was over and the results were no good. To the staff of the Census Bureau, we were just completing the first month of a six-month census-taking process, though admittedly the first month hadn't been as successful as we had hoped.

The headlines and the hearings created a difficult environment in which to recruit additional census takers and to motivate our 340,000 temporary workers (the peak work force in May of the half million over the year). Nevertheless, faced with over 30 million households to call on, including the unanticipated extra 6 million, it took us only three extra weeks beyond the planned six weeks to do the follow-up. We coached census takers to be persuasive, yet polite. Patience and persistence are virtues in census taking. Enumerators needed both:

• Enumerator Lynn Beverly knocked at the door of a house in Compton, California. The door opened, and there stood a naked man. "I said, 'Sir, would you put your clothes on?'" Beverly recalled. "He said, 'No. If you count me, you have to count me as I am.'" She did.

• In northern Michigan, an amorous moose diverted a census taker from her rounds. Two other enumerators were forced to take evasive action after meeting a bear.

• Enumerator Sharyn Leonard's car broke down while returning from counting people in the remote stretches of Nevada. She spent a cold night in the Black Rock Desert, fending off circling coyotes. "I always wanted to travel, but this isn't what I had in mind," she said.

• Census takers Howard and Georgia Kahn took shelter in an abandoned trailer after their car ran out of gas in the wilds of Oregon. They survived for three days on spring water and peanut butter before they were rescued.

• An Alton, Illinois, woman mistook an enumerator for a fund raiser and bit the census taker on the shoulder.

• A homeowner in Monticello, Mississippi, shot and wounded census taker Harmon Broome, thinking he was a trouble-making teen. Fortunately, Mr. Broome recovered. Thankfully, no one else was seriously hurt in the 1990 census, although Mr. Broome wasn't the only census taker shot at.

In addition to the difficulty the bureau had recruiting census takers, we also had problems with the address lists. Some houses and apartment buildings were assigned to the wrong blocks; some new homes were not on any address list; demolished buildings still appeared on the rolls; many multiple-unit buildings were listed as single-family homes because of illegal conversions by owners or landlords.

Illegal conversions proved to be a big problem all over the country, from the quintessential East Coast suburb of Levittown, New York, to big-city neighborhoods in East Los Angeles. In New York and other large cities with serious housing shortages, families, friends, and even strangers were doubled and tripled up in apartments in clear violation of their leases.

In fact, many of the people missed by census takers live in households that are counted by the census. One census worker told of standing in an apartment obviously occupied by three families. Yet the woman who answered the door claimed that only she and her two children lived there. The rest were "just visiting," she said. Ethnographic researchers with whom the Census Bureau contracted to help identify potential problems in getting a complete count found 10 to 12 people living in two- and three-bedroom apartments in New York City's Chinatown.

Language is another challenge. Fourteen percent of U.S. residents speak a language other than English at home. There are millions of people who are not fluent in English. As a practical matter, the bureau printed questionnaires only in English and Spanish. But there were information guides in 32 languages, including Yiddish. The Census Bureau's Yiddish, however, triggered *kvelling* and *kvetching* for its grammatical lapses and fractured vocabulary.

Not Now, I'm Busy

The Census Bureau cannot count people who do not want to be counted. The cities and special-interest groups who sue the bureau because it misses people have themselves failed to convince many in their own communities to stand up and be counted.

While non-response was highest among Blacks, Hispanics, American Indians, and renters, the 1990 census encountered resistance even in such yuppie enclaves as Fairfield County, Connecticut.

"Middle class takes a pass on census," read a *USA Today* headline. While exaggerating the problem, the story accurately reported resistance in upscale, White communities, such as Palm Springs, California, Chicago's West Side, and Manhattan's upper East Side—where the rich pay doormen to guard their privacy. Here's a look at some of the resisters:

• In suburban New Jersey, an insurance executive, realizing the importance of the census for reapportionment and government funding, completed his form with one omission—income. Despite the bureau's confidentiality pledge, he thought this information would be shared with other government agencies such as the Internal Revenue Service. (He was wrong.)

• On the David Brinkley show on April 15, TV personality Barbara Walters acknowledged that she hadn't returned her census form. Her excuse: she did not have a lead pencil. Another of her problems: "it's too tough," she said. If Barbara Walters claimed she couldn't handle the census form, imagine the effect on her viewers.

• An editor at a newspaper that had editorialized loudly about the undercount, critical of the bureau's effort, admitted to a colleague that she had not filled out her questionnaire. She was busy and hadn't gotten around to it, she said. Besides, the form was too long and looked like a bother.

• In South Boston, a man burst out of his front door at the sight of the census taker, who was there only because he had failed to return his questionnaire. "I'm not telling you anything but my name and address. That's all you need to know," he said belligerently.

• A completed census questionnaire arrived in my office in 1992, not two years late for the 1990 census but 32 years late for the 1960 census! That year, the form told respondents: "DO NOT MAIL—HAVE READY FOR CENSUS TAKERS." Apparently, this citizen had waited in vain for over three decades. It was much too late to add the information on this form to the 1960 census count. And I can't to this day reveal the name of the individual who sent in this form—that's confidential until 2032.

• In Orange County, California, Lawrence Samuels—a libertarian—headed up the Voluntary Census Committee with the goal to make the census voluntary. "Every year, they keep adding a few more questions, invade a little more privacy," Samuels told *USA Today*, not saying whether or not he was "volunteering" to answer the census.

For Mr. Samuels, this resistance may be a political statement. But he and others who fail to mail back their census questionnaires are a financial burden for the rest of us.

Despite these obstacles, secretary of commerce Mosbacher announced on July 1, 1990, that the census had counted every known housing unit. The people living in each unit had been enumerated or enumerators had determined that the unit was vacant. This did not mean that the bureau knew of every housing unit in the U.S. That's impossible, no matter how much effort goes into building an address list. There are too many unusual housing units ever to know of all of them—such as converted attics and basements, tents in the woods, or recreational vehicles on the move.

Because of the difficulty in tracking down every housing unit, the Census Bureau does more than the primary census count—which includes mailing out the questionnaire and house calls to households that do not return their questionnaire or do not have a mailable address. The 1990 primary count covered 96 percent of the population. An additional 2 percent were counted through a half-dozen coverage improvement efforts that took place from July through October of 1990. The final 2 percent remained uncounted. Two of the coverage improvement efforts will live long in my memory: local government review and the "Were You Counted?" campaign. Both revealed the difficulties of accurately counting a hostile public when money and power are at stake.

Local Government Review

Local review was supposed to be a cooperative venture between the Census Bureau and the nation's 39,189 units of local government. The Census Bureau gave each government a last chance to examine the bureau's housing unit counts on a block-by-block basis. Governments were to alert the bureau if housing unit numbers did not match their official records. The bureau promised to send census takers out to recheck blocks in which local governments found discrepancies.

When my communications aide, John Connolly, and I heard about these plans, we knew the bureau was setting a course for a public relations disaster. Because other coverage improvement efforts were still in progress, the counts sent by the bureau to local governments were preliminary, not complete. The bureau would add more people to the count before it was delivered to President Bush on December 31.

"I can't believe these people," said Connolly, referring to the bureau staff who planned local review. "Every morning they lay out their pistols, rifles, shotguns, and AK-47s and ask, 'Which shall I shoot myself in the foot with today?'"

Our foreboding was not misplaced. Local governments, with whom the bureau was trying to cement good relations, instead tried to bury us in cement. With federal dollars riding on every person, most governments were certain that their populations were undercounted.

The problem is that the Census Bureau does not do things the way cities want them done. Each city wanted a list of actual addresses with the number of people living at each address, making it easy for them to check against their records. But this detailed information was confidential. Instead, the bureau gave maps to each local government that showed the blocks in its jurisdiction, the number of housing units on each block, and the total population count for the governmental unit.

Each government had been allowed this same sort of local review before the census started, when we were improving address lists. After that review, the bureau had not told local governments whether it had added any of the housing units to the mailing lists that local governments claimed the bureau had missed. In fact, the bureau had added the missing units to the lists. This lack of communication had created some bad feeling toward the bureau in local governments across the country.

During the post-censal local review, each government had three weeks to compare numbers and complain. It didn't take them long to complain. The complaints went first to local newspapers, then to us. Overall, 17 percent of local governments, including the 51 largest cities in the country, challenged our counts. Seven cities claimed an undercount of housing units on more than 2,000 blocks. New York City and Chicago protested our housing unit counts on over 11,000 blocks each! On September 20, the front page of *The New York Times* bore a photograph of a large apartment building in Sunnyside, Queens, with the city's claim that this was one of the 254,534 housing units missed by the Census Bureau. [14]

We had to honor our pledge to recheck every block on which a local government claimed a discrepancy, though some of those claims (such as missing one-quarter of a million housing units in New York City) were preposterous.

"We didn't hire blind persons as enumerators!" exclaimed Charlie Jones, the Census Bureau staffer in charge of the census. (The Census Bureau does hire the blind for other positions.)

"Send census workers out, but let's check a few of the claims ourselves," I decided. Eighteen of us, including Under Secretary Darby, fanned out to ten cities.

The beach at Gateway National Recreation Area in Queens was deserted when our observers got there, except for an overturned lifeguard stand. The 414 apartments that the City of New York claimed existed in block 217, tract 972, were not in evidence on the sandy beach. Suzanne Howard, an assistant deputy secretary in the Commerce Department, could not find the 1,386 additional apartments that the city claimed were in the block containing the Empire State building, where the census had already counted 512 apartments. After talking to building managers and postal carriers, she determined that no part of the Empire State building is residential. The only other building on the block has 688 rental units, but over 150 of them are offices or stores.

Nor did we find 503 occupied apartments in a square block in the Bronx where the census counted only 83. I did have some doubts, however, as I drove up the hill to it, again, as on S-Night, in the company of Sheila Grimm, New York's regional census director. We both gulped as a block loomed ahead of us that obviously had more than 83 apartments. Up close, however, it proved to be one of the many windowless, abandoned blocks of the Bronx. The block was being renovated. Sheila, sleuth that she is, found the office of the contractor.

"Eighty-three sounds about like the number of apartments finished and occupied last April 1," an office manager confirmed for us, "but more are coming on line daily," he said proudly.

Our New York City re-review of local review was not unique. John Connolly checked up on census block 401 in census tract 701 where his old home town, the City of Boston, claimed we missed 373 housing units. The block turned out to be on Boston Common!

In the Chicago Loop, Chicago claimed we missed 283 units in block 204. But this proved to be an all-commercial block consisting of the former Essex Inn, the Johnson Publishing Company (of *Ebony* and *Jet* fame), and a YWCA.

Detroit complained that we missed 279 units on what turned out to be a grassy median across from Palmer Park. It also claimed we missed 171 units in a block in the process of being converted to residential units, but which were not open as of April 1, 1990. The city probably had issued building permits for the conversions and treated them on its records as occupied.

In Baltimore, Under Secretary Darby found a block in which the city claimed there were 98 units. But it was a newly constructed park.

In all, the Census Bureau recanvassed 20 percent of the blocks in the nation. Across the country, local government records proved to be out of date. Many cities assumed that building permits issued were buildings occupied as of April 1. Buildings that had been torn down remained on city rolls. Cities count jails, nursing homes, and hospitals by the number of beds in them, not the number in use at census time.

But the cities did have some legitimate gripes. Many of the discrepancies they found turned out to be geographic coding errors in the TIGER system, in use for the first time. The occupants of the building in Sunnyside, Queens, which made the front page of the *Times,* had been counted. But for some reason the building had been coded into the wrong block. The housing unit counts that the bureau sent New York City listed nothing on the block that was supposed to have the Sunnyside building, but far too many housing units for the block across the street. Of course New York did not tell us about the overcount of housing units on the facing block.

Such errors caused many cities to howl, and rightfully so. The geographic coding errors were ours. Once we fixed them, we found few uncounted housing units as a result of local review. For all the bad press it generated and money it cost, local review added only 0.2 percent to the count. The technical errors were impossible to explain to the public. Many city leaders refused to believe that we corrected the mistakes. In addition, both the bureau and the cities know that counting a housing unit does not mean everyone living there came forth to be counted. Perhaps the only real benefit of local review was that we could correct the geographical errors we found in the TIGER system, and thus the data will be entered correctly into the master address file for census 2000.

Were You Counted?

"Were You Counted?" was a follow-up campaign to flush out those who thought they might have been missed by the census and wanted to be counted. The bureau designed a questionnaire that anyone could reprint and distribute. It asked the same questions as the census short form, but put them on a single sheet of paper that could be printed in a newspaper, distributed as a flyer, or handed out at a state fair or other community event.

New York City, still convinced that the census address lists were inadequate and many of its constituents uncounted, distributed over 100,000 "Were You Counted?" questionnaires during the first two weeks of July in the Sunday editions of *New York City, The New York Times, The Daily News,* and *Newsday.*[15] Few were returned. Spanish-language versions were handed out at festivals in California by Latino volunteers. Some of the 50,000 cooperating community groups and complete-count committees reprinted and distributed the forms at fairs, July 4th events, and in public places across America.

So as not to count anyone twice, whenever a "Were You Counted?" form came into the bureau, we used special scanners to determine whether we had already received a questionnaire from that address. If so, we checked the names on the form against those on the original questionnaire. We added addresses and names to the 1990 census count only if the address on the "Were You Counted?" form was not on our list, or the original questionnaire from that address did not include one or more of the names on the form. It turned out the bureau had already counted two-thirds of those who sent in "Were You Counted?" forms.

It was in Detroit, not New York City, where "Were You Counted?" forms hit the fan. Mayor Coleman Young went into orbit when the local review count for Motown came in 30,000 below the 1 million mark. The Census Bureau's regional director, Dwight Dean, and I explained to the Mayor that other follow-up operations still under way might push Detroit's final tally over 1 million.

But Mayor Young had reason to worry. For 20 years, his had been a shrinking city with an unusual problem. Over the years, the Michigan state legislature has written over 20 laws giving special privileges to "cities of one million or more." One of these laws, for example, allows an income tax on those who work in the city but live in the suburbs. The problem is that Detroit is the only city of that size in Michigan. The laws were worded in that way to appease legislators from outside the city who did not want to give special privileges to Detroit. [16]

Mayor Young looked at the local review figures, asked the city planning department to challenge the count on 7,581 blocks, then assigned city employees to conduct an aggressive "Were You Counted?" campaign.

Mayor Young's somewhat overzealous employees, including those in uniform, turned in 88,525 "Were You Counted?" forms with 154,412 names on them. We field checked these and ended up adding 47,109 persons to the count, or 30 percent of the additional names. Among those we did not include, 56 percent were names we had already counted. Among the remaining addresses and names, we found parking lots (701), housing units that had been demolished (236), non-existent addresses (1,115), the names of people who did not live at the address or were confirmed dead (722), and the names of people who were unknown to those living at the address (2,512). A lot of creative writing had gone into filling out "Were You Counted?" forms in Detroit.

Mayor Young did get his wish, however: The many coverage-improvement operations pushed Detroit's final population count to 1,027,000.

Mayor Young and I will forever disagree about the 107,000 people listed on those forms who we refused to add to Detroit's count, determining that they had already been counted or were fictitious. Young was convinced that Detroit's population was 1.1 million, and nothing less would satisfy him. In July 1991, Mayor Young and his city sued the Department of Commerce and the Census Bureau for wrongful enumeration and statistical adjustment (as he had sued on census day 1980). On September 23, 1993, the Sixth Circuit Court unanimously upheld the District Court's judgment in favor of the Commerce Department and the Census Bureau. I claim Detroit was thoroughly counted, and the court agreed.

By 1992, according to Census Bureau population estimates, Detroit's population had slipped by another 16,000. I wish Mayor Dennis Archer well—he succeeded the 20-year incumbency of Mayor Young in 1994. But my advice to him is to work with the Michigan legislature to change the wording of the laws from "1 million" to "750,000."

A Court Fight

The Constitution requires that the census count and apportionment figures be delivered to the president of the United States within six months of census day. Because census day is April 1, census results historically have been delivered on December 31. Until 1990, that is.

The media never figured out why we surprised them with census numbers the day after Christmas. Most of those covering the bureau beat were enjoying a day off, anticipating the big story to come five days later.

I had been warned. A year earlier in my briefing with former Census Bureau director Vince Barabba, he had given me a graphic description of what happened in 1980 when he nearly became the first director not to deliver the count on time. A lower court had decided in favor of New York City in its lawsuit against the bureau demanding adjustment of the city's count (Carey, Koch et al. vs. Klutznick, Barabba, et al.). At issue in the case was access to the Census Bureau's address register, which Barabba and the bureau had denied. Detroit had also won its demand for adjustment at the lower-court level. The Census Bureau was appealing both cases, in the New York case to the United States Court of Appeals for the Second Circuit and in the Detroit case to the Sixth Circuit.

On December 29—two days before the census count was due at the White House—the United States District Court for the Southern District of New York "Ordered, Adjudged and Decreed that defendants (Census Bureau/Commerce) adjust population figures for 1980 for New York State and its subdivisions and New York City in particular...and that defendants are restrained from certifying population totals for New York to the president on or before December 31, 1980, or thereafter until such time as they have fully complied with this judgment."

Having already decided that statistical adjustment for an overall net undercount of 1.2 percent was impossible to do using the statistical tools of that time, the Census Bureau and Commerce Department headed for the Supreme Court. On the night of December 30, the Supreme Court issued a stay of the Southern District of New York's order preventing delivery of the count. The Supreme Court had already delivered such a stay in the Detroit case. Both stays were pending appeal to their respective Circuit Courts. The two Circuit Courts finally determined both of these cases in favor of the Census Bureau, but it took until the middle of the 1980s for them to do so. Had the Supreme Court not overturned the order blocking certification of the numbers, the 1980 census could not have been delivered before it was obsolete.

As *The New York Times* reported in an article dated December 31, "After the most tortured census in American history, plagued by bitter lawsuits, the Census Bureau officially certified the 1980 population count of the states today and reported it to President Carter only hours before the legal deadline." [17]

As my deadline neared for 1990, I was determined to avoid a repeat of the 1980 problems. New York City's lawsuit wasn't a threat. It was on hold following a stipulation in 1989 that the decision on whether to adjust the census would be based on findings from the post-enumeration survey to be analyzed in 1991. This time there was no threat from the Big Apple.

By now, however, a number of lawsuits had been filed (the final total for the 1990 census would be 21), most of them claiming undercount. The most ominous rumblings were from the South— Georgia and Texas. I had visions—nightmares might be the more descriptive term—of Atlanta or Texas doing to me what New York tried to do to Barabba. I shared my worries only with Under Secretary Darby and a few of my colleagues at the bureau.

"Like the vintners who will serve no wine before its time," said Louis Kincannon, the bureau's deputy director, "the Census Bureau releases no statistic before its time." By "its time" he meant after every known check of accuracy and validity is complete.

The Census Bureau builds a block of time into the decennial census schedule during which the bureau's Population Division reviews the population counts on its computer screens. Specialists in the Population Division compare the count for each unit of local government with its prior census count, with its between-census population estimates (which are based on vital statistics such as birth and death records), with construction permit data collected by the Census Bureau, and, if necessary, with what professionals at census regional offices know about population growth or loss in the area. As the deadline for 1990 delivery neared, the Population Division was certifying the counts, one by one, for each of the 39,189 local government units.

Early on the morning of December 26, Paula Schneider, the chief of the Population Division, informed me that her staff had worked until late on Christmas Eve and the end was in sight. Nothing more remained to be done to complete the 1990 census except to merge the overseas count (military and federal employees and dependents) with the 50-state count. We kept the two counts separate until the very end to prevent any leak of final population and apportionment figures before they reached the president. This merge could be done and final numbers produced with just two hours' notice. The 1990 census was a statistic whose time had come.

I called Darby. "Let's roll it. There are no injunctions now, why risk them in the next few days?" I said.

"I've got to check that the secretary and the White House are prepared to receive the census numbers," he said. Within half an hour he called with the go-ahead.

"Merge the two counts and run the apportionment figures," I told the Population Division.

And that's why President Bush received the 1990 census population count of 249,632,692 and the population counts and reapportioned number of representatives for each state at 1:30 on the afternoon of December 26, five days ahead of schedule. Once I confirmed that the count was at the White House, I called our oversight chairmen, Rep. Sawyer and Senator Kohl, and told them.

By 3:00 P.M., Darby and I stood in front of a room full of reporters who had scrambled to the hastily called press conference after being tracked down by their editors. Felicity Barringer of *The New York Times* just made it after corralling a baby-sitter to watch her child. Several other reporters were routed from Christmas vacations. One census reporter who was not in attendance was my co-author, then with *USA Today*. Reached in New Jersey where he had gone for Christmas, he was breaking the speed limit on the New Jersey Turnpike as he raced back to Washington. He filed background material from pay phones along I-95, while a *USA Today* colleague covered the press conference.

The results of the 1990 census led the network evening news on ABC, CBS, NBC, and CNN. It was the lead story the next day on the front pages of America's 1,600 daily newspapers. Little did the public know how rocky the road had been to that day. Little did I know how rocky the road would be from that day forward.

"The United States has an excellent census that counts nearly everyone," reports author Harvey Choldin of the University of Illinois in his book, *Looking for the Last Percent*. [18] Unfortunately, "nearly everyone" is not enough for the critics.

References

1. Kulka, Richard A., Nicholas A. Holt, Woody Carter and Kathryn L. Dowd (1991). "Self-Reports of Time Pressures, Concerns for Privacy, and Participation in the 1990 Mail Census," *Proceedings, 1991 Annual Research Conference* (Washington, D.C.: Bureau of the Census, 1991), p. 53.

2. Fay, Robert E., Nancy Bates and Jeffrey C. Moore (1991). "Lower Mail Response Rates in the 1990 Census: A Preliminary Interpretation," *Proceedings, 1991 Annual Research Conference* (Washington D.C.: Bureau of the Census, 1991), pp. 23-25, 31.

3. Kulka, pp. 38, 53.

4. Fay, p. 26.

5. Kulka, p. 44.

6. Singer, Eleanor, Nancy A. Mathiowetz, Mick P. Couper (1993). "The Impact of Privacy and Confidentiality Concerns on Survey Participation: The Case of the 1990 Census," *Public Opinion Quarterly*, Winter 1993, 57, 4, pp. 465-482.

7. *Ibid*, p. 53.

8. Fay, p. 19, reporting on the study by Kulka and NORC.

9. *Ibid*, p. 27.

10. *Ibid*, p. 9.

11. *Ibid*, p. 28.

12. Kulka, pp. 40-43.

13. "Grapevine," *Time*, April 23, 1990, p. 21.

14. Levine, Richard (1990). "New York Claims Census Missed 254,534 Abodes," *The New York Times,* September 20, 1990, p. A1.

15. Mireya, Navarro (1990). "Short Census Form Will Be Included in New York Newspapers," *The New York Times,* June 29, 1990, p. B4.

16. Wilkerson, Isabel (1990). "Detroit Desperately Searches for Its Very Lifeblood: People," *The New York Times,* September 6, 1990, p. A1.

17. Reinhold, Robert (1981). "1980 Census Figures Reported to Carter Near the Deadline," *The New York Times,* January 1, 1981, p. A1.

18. Choldin, Harvey (1994). *Looking for the Last Percent,* (New Brunswick, New Jersey: Rutgers University Press, 1994), p. 227.

CHAPTER 9

Adjusting the Census: Adding Estimation

Judge Joseph M. McLaughlin of Federal District Court in Brooklyn enrolled me in a graduate course in statistics. He didn't know it and may not to this day. Nor did I know it when he handed down the Stipulation and Order in the summer of 1989 in the adjustment lawsuit, formally known as The City of New York et al., Plaintiffs, vs. United States Department of Commerce et al., Defendants. When I was appointed census director, I became one of the "als," third on the list of names after the secretary and under secretary for economic affairs of the Department of Commerce. I inherited that dubious honor from my predecessor, John Keane, whose name appeared on the lawsuit when it was first filed in 1988.

The lawsuit sought to compel the Department of Commerce and the Census Bureau to correct the 1990 census to compensate for any undercount. Such a suit was all but inevitable, provoked by the Commerce Department's 1987 decision not to adjust—i.e., correct—the census, although methods to do so had been under study at the bureau throughout the 1980s. It also foreshadowed the problems to come in taking the 1990 census, which found a growing number of Americans ignoring or avoiding census enumeration. This is why building an estimate of those missed into the census count is necessary for an accurate measure of the population in the future. It was so in 1990, and it will be even more so in censuses to come. It may not be the perfect solution—

100 percent cooperation would be more desirable—but it is the practical solution in an imperfect world.

For a legal document, Judge McLaughlin's stipulation was fairly simple and straightforward, running to six and one-fourth pages of readable directions, binding on both parties, with relatively few "whereas" paragraphs. To paraphrase the stipulation, it said the following:

• The Commerce Department's 1987 decision against statistical adjustment or correction for undercount or overcount in the 1990 decennial census is vacated.

• The Census Bureau will undertake a post-enumeration survey of at least 150,000 households to ensure the possibility of using the results not solely for evaluation purposes, as originally planned, but also to produce corrected counts that could be used for all purposes for which the bureau publishes data.

• The Commerce Department is to develop statistical and policy guidelines for deciding whether to adjust, which are to be published by March 10, 1990.

• Using the guidelines, if the secretary determines to adjust, the bureau must publish corrected population data no later than July 15, 1991. If he decides not to adjust, by that date he must make a detailed statement of the grounds for the decision and which guidelines weren't met.

• The Census Bureau and Commerce Department may report census counts in accordance with dates set forth in Title 13 (the census law requiring counts to be delivered to the president by December 31, 1990), but all published counts must bear the legend that they are subject to correction up until July 31, 1991.

• The defendants must establish an independent advisory panel of eight to advise them. (Four to be nominated by the Commerce Department, four by the plaintiffs).[1]

This stipulation was agreed upon a few weeks before I made my decision to accept the nomination for census director. It was a factor in my decision. In my 25 years of doing survey research, first in graduate school and then in the private sector, I had been a let-the-data-decide person. I always tried to design studies that were as objective and unbiased as possible, then drew conclusions, suggested strategies, and recommended decisions to clients based on what the data from the studies showed. This is the only way to survive in the survey research field.

With that background and philosophy, I was open to whatever the post-enumeration survey results showed. If the results showed little undercount, too small to correct, then I would not recommend adjustment. If they showed that adjustment could improve accuracy, then I would recommend it. In my final job interview with Secretary Mosbacher he made it clear to me that—although he reserved the final decision to himself in the court stipulation—I was to give him my best judgment on what the decision should be. He, in turn, might or might not accept my recommendation, but he would give it serious consideration. I believed then that Mosbacher meant what he said. I still do.

Shattered Optimism

As the census began, it was fairly clear who was for and who against adjustment. Those in favor and those opposed were identified and quoted frequently by the press, they were apparent at Congressional hearings. In general, Democrats favored adjustment, especially those representing large urban areas in the Northeast and Midwest. So did Blacks, Hispanics, and the organizations that represented them.

Republicans tended to oppose adjustment, particularly those representing suburban and rural areas and the West. The South was generally quiet, except for Dade County, Florida, with its powerful Hispanic population that favored adjustment. The New York City lawsuit boiled down to a coalition of areas dominated by Democrats against a Republican administration represented by the Department of Commerce.

Those against adjustment argued the fairness issue: people who avoid the census are like those who fail to vote. Their voices are not heard. Just as we don't track down people who don't vote, neither should we adjust for those not counted. The problem with this analogy is that those who aren't counted hurt their states and communities because those areas lose political and financial power. They are a burden to others who do their duty and fill out their census forms.

I believed the data could decide this issue as I came to grips with my new post at the Census Bureau. I knew it was impossible to count 100 percent of the population, no matter how much money and time we spent trying to do so. But I was also confident that the census undercount would be no greater and possibly lower in 1990 than in 1980. Most important, I believed that the differential undercount—the difference in the undercount among racial and ethnic groups—would be lower in 1990 than in 1980. The bureau was working intelligently to close the gap, using 1980 research to pinpoint the types of people who go uncounted and directing extra resources—both publicity and enumeration efforts—at them.

As Peter Bounpane, assistant director of the Census Bureau for the decennial census, told me early on, this was why the bureau had boosted its outreach campaign using census-awareness specialists in local communities; this was why 800-numbers were set up to offer help in Spanish and four Asian languages; this was why the bureau worked closely with groups like the NAACP, the League of United Latin American Citizens, and the Mexican American Legal Defense Fund—the first two of which were among the plaintiffs in the New York City lawsuit. And this is why I testified repeatedly at Congressional hearings that we were tackling the differential undercount problem, and that I was optimistic about reducing it.

Every census has had an undercount problem, though only in recent censuses have we known precisely how big a problem. George Washington believed there was an undercount in the first census, taken in 1790. He blamed "the indolence of the mass and want of activity in many of the deputy enumerators," as well as intentional under-reporting by citizens fearing results would be the basis of a new tax. But Washington had no data to back him up.

Since the 1940 census, the Census Bureau has had data showing an undercount. These data come from what is called demographic analysis—which is an analysis of other government statistics, such as records of births, deaths, legal immigration, estimates of illegals, Medicare files, and other sources. Bureau researchers compare census counts against these records. Over the decades, this research has shown the undercount to be declining as census-taking procedures improve, down to 1.2 percent in 1980 nationally, although there remained an undercount of 4.5 percent among Blacks and 0.8 percent among non-Blacks, or a differential of 3.7 percentage points. Adjustment could close this gap by adding a statistical estimate of those missed, but would it improve the accuracy of census figures, especially at the local level? That's what I was about to find out.

My post-census graduate course in statistics began in February 1991 when I enrolled as an ex-officio member of the bureau's Undercount Steering Committee (USC). I was not expected to do the research, but I was expected to understand the results. While the USC would advise me, only I was empowered to make a recommendation to the secretary.

Measuring the 1990 Undercount: Demographic Analysis

The demographic analysis specialists, led by Census Bureau demographer Dr. J. Gregory Robinson, gave us results first.[2]

They shattered my optimism. While their analysis showed that the net census count was good—we had counted 98.2 percent of the population—it was not as good as in 1980, when we had counted 98.8 percent. Even more disappointing, given our efforts to convince diverse groups to be counted, was the increase in the differential undercount between Blacks and non-Blacks to 4.4 percentage points. This was the largest differential discovered since the bureau started measuring differentials with the 1940 census.

It wasn't much of a stretch to understand these numbers. The fact that proportionally more Blacks than Whites remained uncounted was a fairly compelling reason for adjustment. I was beginning to let the data decide.

Estimated undercount by race in the censuses of 1940-1990 according to demographic analysis

	1940	1950	1960	1970	1980	1990
Total population	5.4%	4.1%	3.1%	2.7%	1.2%	1.8%
Non-Blacks	5.0	3.8	2.7	2.2	0.8	1.3
Blacks	8.4	7.5	6.6	6.5	4.5	5.7
Percentage Point Difference (Blacks minus non-Blacks)	3.4	3.8	3.9	4.3	3.7	4.4

Source: Bureau of the Census, 1991

There was no way we could use the results from this demographic analysis to adjust the census because the data were national in scope. To adjust the census, we needed geographically detailed data on the undercount. To do that, we needed many more statistics.

Measuring the 1990 Undercount: The Post-Enumeration Survey

More statistics are what we got from the Census Bureau's Dr. Robert Fay, John Thompson, Dr. Mary Mulry, and an army of statisticians, including consultants from Harvard, Northwestern, the State University of New York, UCLA, Penn State, and other leading universities. These experts presented us with geographically and demographically detailed data on the undercount based on the post-enumeration survey (PES) of the population. Now things were getting much more difficult.[3]

While the Census Bureau had experimented with post-enumeration surveys before, the results always contained more error than the undercount they aimed to fix. Was the 1990 post-enumeration survey accurate enough to use for adjustment? That's what I needed to determine. It certainly was the largest sample survey ever done by the Census Bureau, and it was probably the most accurate.

The 1990 PES started with a sample of 5,000 blocks, including proportionately more blocks in which hard-to-count people live. The most competent census enumerators were sent to interview all 170,000 households on those blocks, counting over 400,000 people, completing the survey at all but 1.4 percent of the households in the sample.

The Census Bureau then matched the people counted in the PES with those counted by the census. This was first done by computer. Then bureau analysts examined each case the computer could not match. By comparing the names of those counted in the census with the names of those counted in the post-enumeration survey, the bureau estimated the number of people missed, their demographic characteristics, and where they lived.

In the 1980 post-enumeration survey, the quality of the name-matching procedure was questionable. This was why the bureau could not use those data for adjustment. The computer-matching techniques were much better in the 1990 post-enumeration survey, in part because enumerators were told to pay special attention to collecting names accurately and in part because computer software for name matching had come a long way in ten years.

But were the results accurate enough to correct the small undercount? It is very difficult to improve on a count of 250,000,000 using a survey of 400,000.

It was a long spring. Sometimes I emerged from meetings with the Undercount Steering Committee certain we had solved all the statistical problems. Often I emerged confused. That's when I called in the statistical experts for one-on-one tutoring on variance smoothing, loss-function analysis, and other statistical procedures they were using.

Statistical stress is not listed as an occupational hazard. It should be for the job of census director. The more we learned, the more we wanted to learn. There was always one more computer run to do, one more analysis to perform. But rather than making things clearer, many of the additional tests only raised more questions. Then the USC had to go back to the computers again.

Statisticians like to work with probabilities, not certainties. They enjoy what they do and like doing it—and doing it, and doing it. It was for them that Deputy Director Kincannon came up with his slogan "no statistic before its time."

All of our work confirmed what the demographic analysis had shown. There was an undercount of about 2 percent. In the nonpolitical world of research, this would be considered an amazingly accurate result for a count of such scope and size. The census, however, is in a highly political world.

The post-enumeration survey population estimate (or what was called a dual-system estimate because it was formulated using both the PES and the census) showed that the census had missed 2.1 percent of Americans, similar to the demographic analysis estimate of 1.8 percent missed. Not only were Blacks less well counted than Whites, but so were Hispanics, American Indians, and to a lesser extent Asians. The question now was how to model the undercount to statistically add people to the exact geographic locations where they belonged.

The Census Bureau had already designed such a model. The court stipulation required the bureau to design it before the census. The model divided the population into 1,392 types of people (or "strata") and applied an estimate of the undercount or overcount to every person counted in the census, according to that person's stratum. For example, a young Black man living in rental housing in a Northeastern central city might be in a group that had been undercounted by 5 percent. The adjusted population estimate would count him as 1.05 persons. As a White female homeowner, over age 60, living in the South Atlantic (in Washington, D.C., actually), I was worth about 0.97 of a person in the adjusted estimate.

We weren't the only ones doing research. The other advisory panel members, especially those chosen by the plaintiffs, conducted their own analyses of the post-enumeration survey data. To gain access to these data, advisory panel members had to swear to the same confidentiality oath as census employees do.

And if this wasn't enough, Under Secretary Darby and his deputy Mark Plant were doing their own study. They consulted with professors at the University of California at Berkeley. One of those professors, Dr. David Freedman, has a list of anti-adjustment publications as long or longer than the pro-adjustment publication list of the professors on the plaintiffs' side of the advisory panel.

In all, Commerce Secretary Mosbacher had ten advisors: Under Secretary Darby, eight advisory-panel members, and me. My advice would lean heavily on the work done by the USC and the statisticians backing it up at the Census Bureau—that is, if we could ever finish our study.

The deadline was mid-June for a last meeting of the Undercount Steering Committee. Each of the nine members was to give me his opinion and then write a report on the accuracy of the adjusted population estimate versus the unadjusted census count.[4] One member of the committee, statistician Bob Fay, arrived at the USC meeting wearing a tee shirt from the previous year's American Statistical Association conference. It was emblazoned with the words: "Being a statistician is never having to say I'm certain."

The demographers on the USC actually had an easy time of it. There were identifiable demographic groups among the 1,392 types of persons who were less well counted than others. There was reasonable consistency across the nation in the undercount rate for these groups. Adjustment would markedly improve their counts. The statisticians on the USC who were more comfortable with probabilities than "yes" or "no" decisions had a harder time deciding which was better: adjusting or sticking with the original count.

In their final opinions, seven of the Undercount Steering Committee members said adjustment would improve accuracy; two felt that it would not improve accuracy. I had to weigh these demographic and statistical opinions against the guidelines produced under court order. These included considering the effect on future censuses and the potential for disrupting reapportionment and redistricting—by now well along in many states. Of course, there was also the most important guideline of all: that the census be considered the most accurate count of the population at the national, state, and local levels—unless an adjusted count could be shown to be more accurate.

Most of the members of the USC believed that an adjusted count would be more accurate. I had reviewed the research as it evolved, listened to their deliberations, and agreed. It was my judgment (with studies to back me up) that if you correct errors at a higher level, you improve things at the lower level.

The Big Decision

On June 28, 1991, two weeks before the decision deadline, I wrote: "As director of the Bureau of the Census, I, Barbara Everitt Bryant, recommend to secretary of commerce Robert A. Mosbacher, that results of the 1990 post-enumeration survey be used to statistically adjust the 1990 census.

"I believe that statistical adjustment, while far from a perfect procedure, will on average increase the accuracy of the 1990 census," I said in my reasoning.

"The Bureau of the Census has measured census undercount since 1940. This undercount is differentially higher for Blacks than non-Blacks, for males than females. It is time to correct this historical problem. Extraordinary efforts were made in 1990 to reduce the differential undercount. The differential was not reduced; in fact it rose slightly. There is no currently identifiable methodology to attain 100 percent population coverage via enumeration in 2000. With the increasing diversity of the country, a growing diversity documented by the 1990 census, the problem could be larger in 2000. Thus correcting for the small percent who can't be reached should be addressed now...Adjusting may bring the numbers closer to the truth but precise truth cannot be measured...Adjustment is an issue about which reasonable men and women and the best statisticians and demographers can disagree...I stand, however, with the majority of the Census Bureau's Undercount Steering Committee in judging that adjustment would improve the 1990 census." [5]

It is now history that Secretary Mosbacher decided against adjusting the 1990 census. His ten advisors split five to five. No member of the advisory panel changed his pre-census opinion for or against adjustment. Under Secretary Darby came down hard in opposition to adjustment, attacking several statistical procedures used by the Undercount Steering Committee. This undoubtedly had some effect in influencing Mosbacher's decision not to adjust the census. Darby is undeniably an expert statistician. He has now returned to his pre-government post as a professor in the Anderson School of Management, University of California at Los Angeles. But I feel that in supporting the anti-adjustment position, Darby looked at the statistical warts on the individual trees in the forest. He missed the big picture: In the forest, parts of some groves were missing.

I recommended one course of action; the secretary of commerce took another. I felt then, and still do today, that the drive for perfection should not stand in the way of improvements. Whether or not to adjust was a close call. Mosbacher jumped in one direction and I in the other. But when we hit the ground, we were not that far apart. I recognize that with his advisors splitting on their recommendation, it would have been hard for him to change 200 years of history. No census has ever been adjusted. Mosbacher worried that doing so would open a door to charges of political manipulation in future censuses. History was against adjustment.

The secretary announced the decision on July 15, 1991, in front of a press corps that had been following the New York lawsuit for three years. He explained how his advisors had split. I was the only one whose position the press hadn't figured out prior to the press conference. As *The New York Times* said that morning, "In making the decision, whose impact is rivaled by its technical complexity, Mr. Mosbacher has been advised by an array of experts. An eight-member panel of non-governmental experts split evenly on whether the count should be adjusted. A nine-member panel of bureau experts split seven-to-two in favor of adjustment...The final recommendation of the Census Bureau director, Barbara Everitt Bryant, could not be learned." [6]

To Mosbacher's credit, he allowed me to make a statement. The press peppered me with questions after our formal statements. The reporters thought I was dead meat, since I was a political appointee who had opposed an important decision of a cabinet officer of the administration. In fact, despite my opposition, I remained the director of the Census Bureau until the day President Bush left office.

"Demographically and statistically, the accuracy of the 1990 census would have been improved by adjustment, and most particularly that adjustment could have corrected the demographically disproportionate undercount of those who either were missed by the census or consciously avoided being counted," I wrote in a magazine article in 1993. [7] I recommended adjustment in 1991, and I still hold that position today.

What was radically different about the 1990-91 adjustment decision," wrote Harvey Choldin in his book, *Looking for the Last Percent*, "was that the Department of Commerce took it away from the bureau and held onto it tightly. Starting in 1987 when the under secretary announced unilaterally that there would be no adjustment in 1990, the department retained control over the decision; the department 'undelegated' it from the bureau." [8]

It is true that I did not have the decision-making authority my predecessor had in 1980 over whether to adjust. But I also feel that the cities, in suing the secretary of commerce, the Department of Commerce, and the Census Bureau in 1980 and 1990, precipitated the department's "takeover" of the Census Bureau. Once the secretary of commerce was sued, the General Counsel's Office at the department had to take on the secretary's defense. The Census Bureau was no longer a quiet statistical agency out in

Maryland, but a problem for the department and its secretary. The lawsuits have diminished the bureau's autonomy, moving adjustment decisions away from the purely statistical arena. But adjustment history is not over.

Court Decisions Go On...and On

New York City et al. went back to court the day after Mosbacher announced his decision. It was two years later in April 1993, and one year after a three-week trial, when Judge Joseph M. McLaughlin handed down his decision upholding Mosbacher's decision. Said the judge:

> ...the court concludes that the secretary's conclusions under each guideline and his ultimate decision against adjustment cannot be characterized as arbitrary or capricious. The breadth of the guidelines left the secretary enormous discretion. Plaintiffs have made a powerful case that the discretion would have been more wisely employed in favor of adjustment. Indeed, were this court called upon to decide this issue *de novo*, I would probably have ordered the adjustment. However, it is not within my province to make such determinations. The question is whether the secretary's decision not to adjust is so beyond the pale of reason as to be arbitrary or capricious. That far I cannot go.

In a footnote, Judge McLaughlin added, "Additionally, I note that in light of recent improvements in statistical tools and the practical benefits that the 1990 PES has provided, the use of adjustment in the next census is probably inevitable." [9]

The Battle Continues

The end of the adjustment debate? Not on your life! New York et al. appealed. Then on August 8, 1994, the U.S. Court of Appeals for the Second Circuit made the same decision about adjusting the 1990 census that I had recommended four years earlier. The court overturned McLaughlin's ruling. It said that the standard by which the decision should be judged was not whether it was arbitrary and capricious, but whether a fundamental right had been denied on the basis of race and ethnicity.[10] The court said that "...the government has not justified its use of 1990 census data that undercounted Blacks and members of other minority groups."[11]

The Commerce Department did not appeal the decision, headed as it was in 1994 by Secretary Ronald Brown who—as chairman of the Democratic National Committee—had thumped for adjustment.

What happens next will take time to sort out. Will there be, for the first time ever, a mid-decade reapportionment using adjusted figures? This would be expensive and unlikely, but possible. Will an adjusted 1990 count become the base upon which annual, updated population estimates are made? This is a more likely scenario that would affect many federal funding programs. Will Wisconsin or Oklahoma, who were interveners in the case, continue to pursue it even though the Commerce Department has chosen not to do so? And how does all this affect decisions about the 2000 census? It may take the Supreme Court to sort it all out.

Back to 1991 and Strange Bedfellows

Shortly before the secretary's decision, the Census Bureau issued a news release showing what the adjusted population estimates would be for states, and for cities and counties with populations of 100,000 or more.

Suddenly, many of those who supported adjustment had second thoughts. Reapportionment consultants quickly figured out that if adjusted counts were used, California and Arizona would each gain a representative in Congress at the expense of Pennsylvania and Wisconsin. State and city officials compared their unadjusted counts with the adjusted estimates and discovered that if adjustment did not raise their share of the population by more than the average undercount rate, adjustment would hurt them. Political power and federal funding are fixed pies, distributed proportionately.

While large cities were less well counted than suburban and rural areas, the big winners in adjustment would be the fast-growing areas of the South and West, not the older Northeastern and Midwestern cities. While New York City would have been slightly better off after adjustment, its gain was far less than it had anticipated. Furthermore, New York State—also a party to the city's lawsuit—would actually lose compared to other states.

They say politics makes strange bedfellows, but now the politicians were jumping out of one bed and into another. They started to panic. Partisan positions fell apart as the battle lines became geographic. In favor of adjustment were the South and West and a few big cities such as New York, Chicago, and Detroit—all in states that would be hurt by adjustment. The Northeast and Midwest now opposed adjustment, preferring the unadjusted census count that maximized their constituencies.

Ironically, secretary of commerce Mosbacher's decision against adjustment worked against Republican state bastions in the South and West. And it pleased those who opposed the administration, the old guard Democrats of the Northeast and Midwest, except those in a few big cities. In the strange world of census politics—just as in the urban versus rural splits of the 1920s, or the slave- and free-state controversies before the Civil War—politicians have a love-hate relationship with the census. [12] Ironically, the politicians would never know there was an undercount if the Census Bureau didn't do the research—the demographic analysis and post-enumeration survey—that uncovers it.

Fortunately, the census has several things working to preserve it: the Constitution requires it, the law protects the census from political tampering, and the professionals at the bureau work tirelessly to produce census data of the highest quality. Without these protections, the nation's leaders would be without the facts they need to make intelligent decisions about our economic and social affairs.

More Statistical Stress

After the secretary's decision on July 15, 1991, I went on to other things. The bureau began its research for census 2000, it began to upgrade its survey-collection methods using computer-assisted tools, and it introduced quality management practices. But my statistical stress didn't end. I faced nearly two more years of it. Court decisions were far in the future. The adjustment issue continued to haunt my tenure as director because Secretary Mosbacher was worried about the differential undercount for which he had refused to adjust.

Mosbacher's concern emerged the day after his decision, on July 16. This was when he, Darby, and I testified at hearings called to explain the decision. The hearings were held by our oversight committees, first the House subcommittee chaired by Rep. Sawyer, then the Senate's census oversight subcommittee chaired by Senator Kohl.

Mosbacher conceded at Sawyer's hearing that, while he had decided not to adjust the census, he might consider adjusting the annual population estimates produced by the Census Bureau in non-census years. The government uses these estimates to distribute many federal funds. Mosbacher proposed that the bureau continue its undercount research, address some of Darby's criticisms, and consider adjusting the annual population estimates.

Now that it was known that adjustment would strip a

representative from Wisconsin, Senator Kohl was clearly on the secretary's side. He wanted the census left alone. Kohl had me on his radar scope as a danger because I had favored adjustment.

Back at the bureau, we reconvened our committee, expanding it to include those who work on population estimates. We called the new committee CAPE—Committee on Adjustment of Postcensal Estimates. Our mission was to decide whether to adjust the 1992 population estimates for the undercount, which were to be released in December 1992.

The bureau produces population estimates by taking the last census count, adding births and immigrants, and subtracting deaths and emigrants. Now we had to decide whether to change the formula, beginning not with the census count, but with the adjusted census estimate.

The data we would use to make the adjustments would come from the post-enumeration survey. But feelings ran high among the committee members that the model used to apply the national undercount rates to local areas could be improved.

We determined that we could produce better estimates of the population by combining strata, estimating and applying undercount rates to different, larger, and therefore fewer categories of people. We also discovered another differential undercount that was as important as the gap between racial and Hispanic groups: housing tenure. The census was much more likely to miss renters than homeowners. After distinguishing renters from homeowners, we ended up with only 357 strata of people instead of the original 1,392.

In re-examining the data, we found that the overall undercount rate was less than we had first calculated. We discovered and corrected a computer coding error, reducing the undercount by 0.4 percentage points. We improved the name-matching procedure and made some other technical changes that cut it by another 0.1 percentage points. The revised undercount was now 1.6 percent rather than 2.1 percent, though gaps between groups persisted. This put the best estimate of the 1990 population at 252,712,821 in the United States, plus the

Estimated net undercount of demographic groups in the 1990 census according to the post-enumeration survey (PES)

	June 1991 original estimate (1,392 post-strata)	August 1992 revised estimate (357 post-strata)	
	undercount	undercount	standard error
Total population	2.08%	1.58%	0.19%
Residents of:			
Owner-occupied housing	n/a	0.07	0.21
Rental housing	n/a	4.31	0.39
Race:			
Non-Blacks	1.69	1.18	0.20
Males	2.02	1.52	0.23
Females	1.36	0.85	0.21
Blacks	4.82	4.43	0.51
Males	5.37	4.90	0.53
Females	4.33	4.01	0.56
Asian/Pacific Islanders	3.08	2.33	1.35
Males	3.54	3.44	1.59
Females	2.64	1.25	1.50
American Indians	4.99	4.52	1.22
Males	5.59	5.18	1.23
Females	4.40	3.86	1.24
Ethnicity:			
Hispanic (of any race)	5.24	4.96	0.73
Males	5.78	5.51	0.90
Females	4.68	4.39	0.71

Source: Bureau of the Census, 1992

922,819 overseas military and federal employees, for a total of 253,735,640. This is 4 million more people than the census counted.

If Mosbacher had decided to adjust the census on that fateful day, these errors meant that we would have added slightly more people to the population than we should have. But even so, the adjusted numbers would have been closer than the census count to our best estimate of the "true" population in an environment where "truth" can never be precisely determined.

More than a year later, CAPE gave me its report.[13] Its research was conclusive. Using newly adjusted figures would improve the accuracy of the national count and counts for most states. It would close the gaps caused by the differential undercount between racial and ethnic groups. It would also improve the accuracy of the proportional distribution of population among most, but not all, states. But below the state level, it was unclear whether the adjusted estimates would be more accurate than the unadjusted counts for local areas.

I planned to make a decision in August. It was a decision that was just as difficult as the one a year earlier. Should I fix the big numbers that are really wrong, at the cost of increasing error at the local level? Or should I ignore the big problems because fixing them might hurt local areas? The adjusted population estimate for Illinois, for example, would reflect the state's true population more accurately than the census count. But in fixing the numbers for the state of Illinois, we might over-adjust Peoria and under-adjust Rockville and not know which was right. Would Americans accept this?

When the CAPE report reached Senator Kohl's subcommittee and the Committee on Governmental Affairs chaired by Ohio Senator John Glenn, the result was explosive. The fireworks intensified when they learned this was no longer a secretarial decision, but had been delegated to me by Commerce Secretary

Barbara Hackman Franklin. Franklin had succeeded Mosbacher, who had left the position to run the Bush re-election team.

The Senators called me to a hearing on August 12, 1992. The tone at this hearing made the 1990 census hearings seem like Sesame Street episodes. The Senators argued that changing the base upon which population estimates are built was a policy decision. They claimed I was treating it as a purely statistical decision, rushing to judgment, and should instead allow input from the public. They assumed I would decide in favor of adjustment because I had done so before. In their view, this would be a bad decision.

At Senator Kohl's request, I delayed my decision to allow time for a public hearing, for publication of *Federal Register* notices about the impending decision, and for public comment. I received letters from 1,118 individuals and organizations. Fewer than 20 had any statistical, demographic, or policy content. The other 1,100 read like fund-raising appeals. Their authors were for or against adjustment based on whether their community would gain or lose. [14]

Over 300 pro-adjustment letters came from Florida alone, including letters from the heads of dozens of correctional institutions, most of whom thought adjustment would help solve their financial problems. Most of the other letters also supported adjustment, which would mean a correction of 1.6 percent nationally. This would have raised the census count of California's share of the national population by 0.14 percentage points, Texas by 0.08 percentage points, and other Sunbelt and Western states by lesser amounts. Pennsylvania's share of the U.S. population would have dropped by 0.06 percentage points, and New Jersey's, Ohio's, and Michigan's by 0.03 percentage points. To a lesser extent, other states in the Northeast and Midwest also would have declined in population share. For 35 of 50 states, adjustment would have made a difference of no more than plus or minus 0.01

percentage points—but when federal funds are involved, states will fight even for one one-hundredth of a percent share of the pie.

On December 29, 1992, I announced my decision. I decided against adjusting the census count as the base for inter-censal population estimates.[15] This may seem inconsistent with my recommendation a year earlier. It may sound as though powerful Midwestern senators on the Governmental Affairs Committee or my own Midwestern roots got to me.

It was neither of these—it was the lawyers. Legal advice from the General Counsel's Office made me overrule my best statistical judgment. The 44,000 cities, towns, townships, counties, metropolitan areas, and states for which the Census Bureau produces population estimates have long been allowed to challenge their estimates. There was no reason, the legal advisors said, that a jurisdiction could not ask for the documentation behind any adjustment. Since we could not prove that by improving a state's estimate, we had made no errors at the local level, the bureau would be tied up for years in hundreds of lawsuits it could not win.

By now the New York suit had been argued, but not yet decided. President Clinton had been elected. My tenure as director would soon end.

It was time for the Census Bureau to move on. We needed to turn our attention to the 2000 census. I could not leave the Census Bureau tied up in legal knots, nor leave my colleagues at the bureau arguing about the past when they should be improving census taking in the future. The future was more important.

I did succeed in leaving one legacy for the U.S. statistical system. While I decided not to adjust census numbers used to produce official, inter-censal population estimates that determine funding, I did allow sponsors of federal surveys conducted by the Census Bureau to calibrate their surveys to the adjusted census estimates if they wanted to do so. I did this because, at the state and large metropolitan area level, I could prove that the adjusted figures were more accurate. Nearly two years after my decision, the Bureau of Labor Statistics got the go-ahead from its general counsel's office that adjusted figures could be used as a base for calibrating the Current Population Survey. Since January 1994, the Current Population Survey—which produces monthly unemployment statistics and annual income and poverty figures—has been based on adjusted population estimates.

No More Two-Number Censuses

I have learned one thing from all the statistical research, political wrangling, nerve-jarring decisions and conflicting court decisions. A two-number census will not work. We cannot have an enumerated count followed later by an adjusted population estimate, as the Census Bureau produced in 1990 and 1991. The two numbers will always set in motion opposing political forces, each promoting numbers that maximize the count to their advantage, and all willing to go to court to try to get the number they want.

The alternative to the two-number census is not the one-number count that has missed people for 200 years. Instead, we need a new one-number census in which estimating non-respondents and the missing becomes a part of census taking. A best-effort enumeration plus estimation would put the count outside politics and back inside the statistical arena. The Census Bureau is researching how to do this now, having experimented with the techniques in the 1995 test census.

This is the way to count an unwilling public, if only the public is willing to accept it.

A Chronology of the 1990
Census Adjustment Decision

Nov. 3, 1988   A year-and-a-half before census day, New York City et al. file a lawsuit demanding adjustment of the 1990 census

July 17, 1989   The U.S. District Court for the Eastern District of New York orders the Commerce Department to vacate its decision not to adjust the 1990 census. It orders the Commerce Department to do a post-enumeration survey, to appoint an expert Special Advisory Panel of eight to advise the secretary of commerce on his decision on whether to adjust the census, and to explain the reasons if he decides not to adjust.

1990   The 1990 census count is delivered. There are 248,709,873 residents in the 50 states and the District of Columbia, plus 922,819 overseas federal employees for a total enumeration of 249,632,692. The Census Bureau conducts the post-enumeration survey.

Spring 1991   Census Bureau research measures the undercount using two methods: Demographic analysis shows a 1.8 percent undercount, while post-enumeration survey analysis shows a 2.1 percent undercount.

June 15, 1991   The court-ordered Special Advisory Panel sends its recommendations to the secretary of commerce. Four are pro-adjustment; four are against adjustment.

June 28, 1991   The director of the Census Bureau recommends adjustment to the secretary of commerce after the Undercount Steering Committee at the Census Bureau votes seven to two that it will improve accuracy.

July 5, 1991   The under secretary of economic affairs recommends against adjustment.

(continued)

169

July 15, 1991   Commerce Secretary Robert Mosbacher decides not to statistically adjust the 1990 census.

After July 15, '91 New York City et al. appeal Mosbacher's decision to the U.S. District Court for the Eastern District of New York.

July 16, 1991   Secretary Mosbacher testifies before the census oversight committees of the House and Senate. He says he will consider adjustment of intercensal population estimates if the Census Bureau can respond adequately to criticism of its adjustment research

May 11, 1992   The three-week trial of New York City et al. vs. the Department of Commerce/Census Bureau begins.

August 1992   Ongoing Census Bureau research revises the postenumeration survey undercount estimate to 1.6 percent. This puts the final best estimate of the resident population of the 50 states plus District of Columbia at 252,712,821, or 4 million more than were enumerated.

Dec. 28, 1992   The director of the Census Bureau decides not to adjust the 1990 census numbers as the basis of official population estimates for non-decennial years. But believing the adjusted census figures are more accurate at state and large-area levels, the director decides to allow sponsors of Census Bureau surveys to use adjusted estimates if they so desire.

April 13, 1993   Joseph McLaughlin, judge of U.S. District Court for the Eastern District of New York, upholds Secretary Mosbacher's decision not to adjust. McLaughlin says the decision was NOT arbitrary or capricious. In a footnote he says if judging *de nova* he might have favored adjustment.

Sept. 24, 1993   New York City et al. appeal the McLaughlin/District Court Decision.

January 1994   The Bureau of Labor Statistics, the sponsor of the Census Bureau-conducted Current Population Survey (CPS), decides to use adjusted 1990 census figures as the basis for calibrating the CPS. Thus, the adjusted census figures become the basis for unemployment statistics, demographic updates, and income and poverty data released by the Census Bureau.

Aug. 8, 1994   The U.S. Court of Appeals for the Second Circuit vacates the decision of Judge McLaughlin/District Court for the Eastern District of New York not to adjust the 1990 census.

Sept. 22, 1994   The Department of Commerce decides NOT to appeal the U.S. Court of Appeals decision, letting the decision stand.

The Future   Uncertain. Perhaps the Supreme Court will decide whether enumerated or statistically adjusted counts should be used now and in the future.

References

1. Stipulation and Order, United States District Court, Eastern District of New York, THE CITY OF NEW YORK, et. al., Plaintiffs vs. UNITED STATES DEPARTMENT OF COMMERCE, et al., Defendants, July 17, 1989.

2. Demographic analysis is described in detail in "Technical Assessment of the Accuracy of Unadjusted Versus Adjusted 1990 Census Counts," Report of the Undercount Steering Committee, Decennial Census Division, (Washington, DC: Bureau of the Census, June 1991).

3. *Ibid.* This report describes the post-enumeration survey as well as demographic analysis.

4. *Ibid.*

5. Barbara Everitt Bryant (1991). "Recommendation to Secretary of Commerce Robert A. Mosbacher on Whether or Not to Adjust the 1990 Census, and Technical Assessment of the Accuracy of Unadjusted Versus Adjusted 1990 Census Counts, Report of the Undercount Steering Committee," (Washington D.C.: Bureau of the Census, June 28, 1991).

6. Barringer, Felicity (1991). "Decision Today on Adjusting the Census," *The New York Times*, July 15, 1991, p. A12.

7. Bryant, Barbara Everitt (1993). "Census Taking for a Litigious, Data-Driven Society," *Chance*, Vol. 6, No. 3, Summer 1993, pp. 44-49.

8. Choldin, Harvey (1994). *Looking for the Last Percent*, (New Brunswick, New Jersey: Rutgers University Press, 1994), pp. 237-238.

9. United States District Court, Eastern District of New York, Memorandum and Order 88 CV 3474, 92 CV 1566, 92 CV 2037, April 13, 1993.

10. U.S. Court of Appeals for the Second Circuit Decision vacating judgment of U.S. District Court for the Eastern District of New York, Docket No. 93-6183, decided August 8, 1994.

11. Rosenbaum, David (1994). "A Likely Long-Term Effect of Census Ruling: More Litigation," *The New York Times*, August 10, 1994, p. A8.

12. Anderson, Margo J. (1988). *The American Census: A Social History* (New Haven, Yale University Press, 1988) describes many of the controversies surrounding the U.S. census throughout its history.

13. Committee on Adjustment of Postcensal Estimates, "Assessment of Accuracy of Adjusted Versus Unadjusted 1990 Census Base for Use in Intercensal Estimates," (Washington, D.C.: Bureau of the Census, August 7, 1992 with Addendum November 25, 1992).

14. Bryant, *Chance*, p. 48.

15. U.S. Bureau of the Census, "Decision of the Director of the Bureau of the Census on Whether to Use Information from the 1990 Post-Enumeration Survey (PES) to Adjust the Base for the Intercensal Population Estimates Produced by the Bureau of the Census," *The Federal Register*, Docket 920895-2347, December 29, 1992.

CHAPTER 10

At Stake: More
Than the Census

"Oh good, you're back from the census," said my friend Joanne, greeting my husband and me as we arrived with our children and grandchildren at Camp Michigania, a summer getaway in northern Michigan where we have vacationed for a number of years.

It was late July of 1991. I had ahead of me just one precious week of rest and relaxation following Secretary Mosbacher's decision not to adjust the 1990 census. I was determined not to look at another number for seven days—unless it was the number of laps for my daily half-mile in the swimming area, or the number of times my grandsons Jake Bryant and Ben Valentine, ages 7 and 6, could hit the bulls-eye in archery. This was likely to be a very small number, something I could cope with on vacation.

Like my friend, many people assumed that with the 1990 census concluded and the decision on adjustment made, I could now come home.

"I'll be back in Washington when the week is over," I told Joanne.

As a census data user for 25 years before I went to the bureau, and as a member of the bureau's marketing advisory committee for six of those years, I was surprised to discover that many people think the Census Bureau shuts down after each census. At one time it did—from the census of 1790 through the census of 1900. Then, as its census and survey work expanded, the bureau became a permanent organization in 1902.

My friend Joanne is not the only person who is unaware of the Census Bureau's many other activities. On May 15, 1994, the day both Hillary Rodham Clinton and I were awarded honorary doctorates from the University of Illinois, I discovered that this lack of awareness occurs in high places. When the First Lady and I were introduced, I told her I had been the director of the Census Bureau for the Bush administration.

"I hope the Clinton administration will replace me soon," I said, referring to the fact that the bureau had been without a director for nearly one and one-half years at that point. "The Census Bureau needs a director."

"But there isn't another census for a long time!" she answered.

I realized then that the First Lady herself was unaware of the bureau's many other important duties. Much of the information used to craft her own health care reform effort—such as the number and characteristics of people who do not have health insurance—came from the Census Bureau's ongoing surveys of the population.

When people learn that the Census Bureau operates throughout the decade, they imagine an army of statisticians and civil servants with little to do. Nothing could be further from the truth.

While there's no ivy on the walls of its headquarters in Suitland, Maryland, the Census Bureau's full-time professional staff of analysts, survey designers, computer scientists, mathematical statisticians, and demographers are like the social sciences faculty at an elite research university. Their names may go unrecognized by the general public, but many analysts at the Bureau publish, teach, present papers at technical conferences, and are recognized among the best in their areas of specialty. They work ceaselessly at collecting and analyzing America's statistics.

"The Census Bureau is like a university without under-graduates or a football team," I said, describing it after I'd been there six months. "But it does have foreign graduate students, libraries, and alumni."

What few realize—and I didn't until after I became direc-tor—is that the Census Bureau has been running an international statistical training program for years. Students from statistical agencies around the world, particularly from less-developed nations, come to the bureau to learn such things as sampling, survey methods, computer processing of census and survey data, and the benefits of providing confidentiality to respon-dents—not yet a worldwide ethic. The international program now has over 6,000 alumni in statistical bureaus around the globe. Along with every Census Bureau retiree and the millions who've worked as enumerators for the last several censuses, these international students consider themselves alumni of the Census Bureau.

I've spent a good portion of my career with "census junk-ies," a term of endearment I use for the hundreds of planners, evaluators, marketers, and policy makers (they weren't called "wonks" until the Clinton administration moved in) who live, breathe, and eat Census Bureau data. Much of those data come not from the decennial census, but from the bureau's other censuses and many surveys of how we live, where we work, what we earn, how much we spend, and how our businesses operate.

Much if not most of what we know about ourselves comes from the Census Bureau. This is why it is not an exaggeration to say that mounting public resistance to the census or refusal to respond to the bureau's other surveys is a threat to our very economic survival. If people refuse to supply the bureau with information about themselves, we will be like the blind men feeling the elephant. We won't see the big picture.

One night in the middle of the month, TV anchorman Dan Rather looks squarely into the camera and comments on the rise or fall of the nation's unemployment rate, "released today by the Bureau of Labor Statistics." Flip the channel and Tom Brokaw is upbeat about the impact on the economy of a rise in "new construction starts," just announced by the Department of Commerce.

The Wall Street Journal offers commentary on the monthly trade balance—how we as a nation are doing on imports and exports—and possible action the administration might take in response to the trade gap with Japan or to news about rising exports to Mexico since NAFTA.

Meanwhile, *USA Today*'s Sam Meddis, who covers the criminal justice system, reports that the Justice Department's Bureau of Criminal Justice Statistics is releasing a report on victims of crime. Policy planners and Congressional representatives examine these data as they consider budget proposals and crime legislation.

What the public doesn't realize—and what commentators and news reports rarely mention—is that all these statistics come directly from surveys conducted by the Census Bureau. The bureau is the survey research arm of the Department of Commerce, collecting the economic indicators that are so important to financial markets. The Census Bureau is also the contract survey research organization for much of the rest of the government. And anyone cruising the Internet can tap into an up-to-the-minute estimate of the current U.S. population from the Census Bureau's population clock.

In a recent and typical year, the bureau performed $39 million worth of surveys for the Bureau of Labor Statistics; $17 million for the National Center for Health Statistics; $13 million for the Bureau of Criminal Justice Statistics; $13 million for the

Department of Housing and Urban Development; and $38 million for other federal agencies and departments. Those expenditures, plus money for censuses and surveys funded through Congressional appropriation, make the Census Bureau the largest survey research organization in the world.

These surveys continue even while the decennial census is under way, although insiders tend to talk about the decennial year and "the other nine years." A drop in the public's response to the Census Bureau's surveys would spell trouble for everyone, from health care planners to the Small Business Administration, from large corporations to convenience stores. Fortunately, such a drop is not occurring—but only because the bureau is running harder and harder just to stay in place.

Working Harder to Get Answers

The largest non-census survey of the American population is the Current Population Survey. From the CPS, as it is called, the Bureau of Labor Statistics extracts much of what we know about the labor force, employment, and unemployment. The Census Bureau, which conducts the CPS, uses the survey findings to keep up to date on American income and poverty levels, educational attainment, marital status, home ownership, childbearing, working mothers, single-parent families, and more. CPS information is vital to policy makers, planners, and businesses. It helps run our free market economy.

In taking the CPS, the Census Bureau interviews 68,000 households each month during the week that includes the 19th. The first result of the CPS is the unemployment rate, announced by the Bureau of Labor Statistics three weeks after the interview week on a date specified a year in advance by the Office of Management and Budget. Until it is released, the unemployment rate is held, as are other economic indicators, under tight security. On the day of its release, the commissioner of the Bureau of Labor Statistics testifies about the rate before the Joint Economic Committee of Congress.

The CPS may not be as big an operation as the census, but it is still a monumental task. To take the CPS, 3,500 interviewers (or field representatives, as they are officially called) fan out across the country equipped with notebook computers. Others work with computer-assisted-telephone-interviewing terminals at central telephone centers in Hagerstown, Maryland; Tucson, Arizona; and Jeffersonville, Indiana (another modern-day task for the site of the Union Army's quartermaster depot). At the end of each day, the field representatives transmit their work by modem to the main database at the Census Bureau. Computer technology has replaced the old-fashioned, tedious, and error-prone process of marking down answers in pencil on paper forms for later tabulation.

In recent years, the bureau's field representatives have had to track down people made homeless by the 1994 Los Angeles earthquake, which occurred during CPS interviewing week. They have also had to cope with the San Francisco earthquake, Hurricane Hugo, and Hurricane Andrew.

Several determined field representatives lost their own homes in Hurricane Andrew, yet still went out and completed their assigned interviews. They visited ruined neighborhoods to try to find those they were assigned to interview. They found them in temporary shelters, emergency camps, and at the homes of friends and relatives.

CPS interviewing is always completed on time because the unemployment rate is a vital national economic indicator. It moves the stock market.

Answering the census is the law. Answering most surveys conducted by the Census Bureau is not. Respondents need to be convinced of the importance of answering questions asked in the Current Population Survey or in one of the approximately 30 to 40 other household surveys the Census Bureau conducts each year. The same 3,500 trained field representatives who collect the CPS responses also do the interviews for other bureau surveys such as the Survey of Income and Program Participation, which probes sources of income, the use of government programs, and people's access to health insurance; the National Health Interview Survey, which asks for more detail about people's health than do their doctors; the American Housing Survey and the metropolitan area housing surveys, which ask about housing; and the Consumer Expenditure Survey, which asks how people spend their money. These surveys are all invasions of privacy to some degree, and all guarantee the confidentiality of your answers. But no law says you have to answer them.

Despite the often personal questions they ask, Census Bureau field representatives get high response rates. With much effort, they've held response rates in the 90 to 95 percent range for the past 20 years for the CPS, the National Health Interview Survey, and the National Crime Victimization Survey. The Consumer Expenditure Survey garners a significantly lower, though still high, response rate of 87 percent, up from the 79 percent of 1980. [1,2,3] Even when people agree to respond to surveys, whether the bureau's or those conducted by academic or private-sector organizations, some refuse to answer questions about income. Many people regard the amount of money they make as a very private subject. On a large consumer survey I directed recently for the University of Michigan, 9 percent refused to provide any details about their income and an additional 4 percent would only answer whether their household income was above or below $30,000.

No other academic or private-sector organization gets response rates close to what the Census Bureau achieves. But in these days of growing public resistance to answering questions, the bureau has had to use all of its strengths to keep response rates up. Fortunately, the Census Bureau has a number of things going for it.

Among the Census Bureau's assets is its confidential list of addresses from the last census, which the bureau uses to select households for surveys. The bureau uses these addresses to send letters to households in advance. These letters explain the importance of the survey and tell householders when they can expect a field representative to call. I signed many such letters during my tenure as director, which the bureau then printed and mailed.

Another important asset of the bureau's is a permanent, trained, professional corps of field representatives who live in or near their interview areas.

A third critical asset is money. The bureau has the funding to follow-up on non-responding households by letter, personal visit, and telephone.

The bureau also has credibility. While the percentage of households that voluntarily mailed back their census form fell in 1990, nearly every household eventually answered the census. Potential respondents know the Census Bureau isn't trying to sell them anything. In contrast, many people distrust surveys fielded by other organizations, fearing they are sales gimmicks in disguise. This lowers response rates.

Response rates are also dropping because it's getting harder for survey organizations to contact people. This is what I'm discovering now that I'm back to doing survey research the usual way—by dialing randomly chosen telephone numbers. Americans have lots of ways of making themselves hard to reach. For a survey I just directed of 210,000 randomly selected telephone numbers from across the nation, 31,000 had answering machines;

5,600 were attached to fax machines or computers; and 41,200 were never answered despite repeated dialing at different times of the day over several weeks. At another 30,300 households, the person answering the phone refused to talk to the interviewer.

The Census Bureau also has problems getting people to respond by telephone. Non-response to its telephone contacts are currently at 15 percent for the CPS and 27 percent for the National Crime Victimization Survey. But the bureau follows up on non-respondents with personal interviews in their homes. This brings final non-response for these surveys down to just 4 or 5 percent.[4]

Other Censuses, More Answers

The Census Bureau also conducts the economic, agriculture, and government censuses every five years. As of the 1992 censuses, these cover 98 percent of economic activity in the nation, collecting data on employment, production, and structural changes in our economy. All of these censuses are conducted by mail at the same time, collecting data for years ending in two and seven.

The economic censuses are actually eight separate censuses, including retailing; wholesaling; the service industries; transportation, communications, and utilities; financial, insurance, and real estate industries; manufacturing; mineral industries; and construction. Results from the economic censuses show that services (including government) now make up 74 percent of our gross domestic product, while manufacturing, agriculture, construction, and mining make up only 26 percent. The agriculture census finds that only 2 percent of the labor force are employed in agriculture, yet those 2 percent produce enough food to feed the United States and export to the rest of the world.

Businesses that answer the economic and agriculture censuses are protected under Title 13. Their identity cannot be revealed for 30 years (compared to 72 for the population). For businesses, the promise of confidentiality is particularly important since their managers do not want competitors to know their sales or other financial data.

In contrast to the confidentiality of the economic and agriculture censuses, the census of governments is not covered by Title 13. That's because the information supplied by state and local governments is publicly available within each jurisdiction.

In addition to these censuses and household surveys, the Census Bureau also fields 125 to 150 business surveys each year, keeping the nation informed about the state of our economy. The surveys include the Annual Survey of Manufacturers, the Annual Retail Trade Survey, the Report of Building or Zoning Permits Issued and Local Public Construction, the Monthly Wholesale Trade Survey, and the Survey of Plant Capacity Utilization. All are closely watched not only by those in the businesses they measure, but also by economists and investors. To do these surveys, the Census Bureau obtains business names and addresses from its Standard Statistical Establishment List, a list developed from surveys and economic censuses of every business establishment (plant, store, etc.) in the U.S. This list contains statistics about each business, such as its address, size, and number of employees. The information in the Standard Statistical Establishment List is completely protected under Title 13.

If a business does not respond to one of its many business surveys, the Census Bureau fills in the blanks with information from tax filings. In fact, the bureau gets much of its data on very small businesses this way to avoid burdening them with paper work. In addition, through the use of technology, the Census Bureau is making it easier for businesses to respond to its surveys. Large retailers can now report their monthly sales by punching in the number on a touch-tone telephone. Some large businesses now transfer data directly from their computers to the Census Bureau, avoiding paperwork entirely.

It is critical for the bureau to get a high response rate to its economic censuses because they benchmark our economic statistics every five years. Response rates to the economic censuses had been falling, from 85 and 86 percent in the censuses of 1972 and 1977, to 83 percent in 1982 and 81 percent in 1987.[5] In the late 1980s, the Census Bureau tackled the falling response issue, determining that one problem was the design of the census forms (there are about 500 different forms for different types of businesses and industries). The Census Bureau redesigned many forms for the 1992 censuses. To determine how to improve response rates, the bureau interviewed businesses and listened to executives in focus groups. Business people told the bureau that they felt overburdened by government reporting, the business equivalent of the invasion of privacy, particularly as they tried to downsize their white-collar staffs. They told the bureau that they would answer its censuses and surveys for only two reasons: (1) if the resulting information would help them understand their own industry and position in it, and (2) if it was the law.

The Census Bureau is always trying to communicate the results of its business censuses and surveys, encouraging people to make more use of the information. And it is the law to answer censuses, although not most surveys. In 1992, for the first time, the Census Bureau mailed its economic censuses questionnaires with the statement, "Your response is required by law," emblazoned on the envelope. It worked. Response to the economic censuses shot up to 89 percent, the highest ever.

Do individuals have as much respect for the law as businesses do? That's one of the questions the 1995 test census will answer. Some of the housing units in the test-census areas received plain envelopes containing their census questionnaire, as in past censuses. Others received envelopes with statements printed on the outside informing residents that response to the census is required by law. The Census Bureau will determine whether the response rate from households receiving "it's the law" envelopes is higher than that of households receiving plain envelopes. If so, Americans will receive their census 2000 questionnaires with "it's the law" reminders printed on the envelopes.

The Census Bureau's Bestseller

Public cooperation with censuses and surveys requires public understanding of what happens to their answers. Not all of us are "census junkies." To spread the results as broadly as possible, the Census Bureau has become one of the largest publishers in the world. It publishes over 1,000 reports in the years following censuses and hundreds of reports in other years. The bureau also makes its data available on computer tapes and CD-ROMs.

The Census Bureau doesn't earn a cent for these publications. All the money goes to the Government Printing Office. The bureau itself sells computer tapes and CD-ROMs, but can only charge for the cost of reproduction. After all, American taxpayers have already paid for the information, so it belongs to them.

The average American most often learns of the results of censuses and surveys through the media. Reporters, editors, and commentators filter what they think is interesting out of the millions of tables produced by the Census Bureau. For those who wonder why the government needs to invade their privacy with a census or survey, look at the fine print at the bottom of a table or chart describing our characteristics or our economy in your local newspaper. The single largest source of information is the Census Bureau.

The Census Bureau publishes a bestseller, one of the longest running books other than the *Bible*, the *Koran*, and *The Old*

Farmer's Almanac (which dates from 1792). It's the annually published *Statistical Abstract of the United States,* first published in 1878. This is a three-pound, over 1,000-page, indexed compendium of statistics from Census Bureau censuses and surveys, from other government agencies, and from dozens of private sources including the National Football League and the American Veterinary Medical Association. The book is crammed with information that ranges from abortion to zinc production. Read it and you can become a master of trivia, as well as of important data.

Read the *Statistical Abstract* and you'll know whether there are more cars in the U.S. than adults (the numbers are close). In Wyoming there are more motor vehicles than people. Read it and you'll know that there are 76 telephones for every 100 people, even more televisions, over two radios for every American, and that U.S. households have more TVs than refrigerators.

The *Statistical Abstract* shows there are over 723,000 lawyers in the United States—more than the population of six of our states. In Washington, D.C., there is one lawyer for every 19 people. Florida has the highest proportion of elderly (18 percent) than any state; it also has the third-fastest-growing population under age five. Nationally, kindergarten through 12th grade enrollment dropped by over 6 million between 1970 and the mid-1980s. It's now rebounding and projected to grow by 8 percent in the decade of the 1990s.

Did you know that 54 percent of the residents of the United States live within 50 miles of a coastline? Or that there are 6 million more women than men, although more male than female babies are born? Or that Asians are the fastest-growing racial/ethnic group? Or that 22 percent of Californians are foreign-born (compared to 8 percent nationally)? These are but a few of the half-million-plus statistics in this fascinating annual publication, the federal government's top-selling book with over 300 million copies sold so far. Librarians report that it is one of the most frequently stolen books—and it is ripped off (legally because the Census Bureau is not allowed to copyright) by a publisher who copies, prints, and sells it for less than what the Government Printing Office charges. The *Statistical Abstract* is the condensed version of everything the Census Bureau has found out in censuses and surveys.

The *Statistical Abstract* also illustrates why it can be difficult to get the public to cooperate with censuses and surveys. There's an oft-told story at the Census Bureau about the respondent who refuses to answer the questions posed by a Census Bureau field representative. "I don't know why the government wastes my time with all these personal questions," the story goes. "You can look up everything you're asking me in the *Statistical Abstract*!"

References

1. Bryant, Barbara Everitt (1990). "Achieving High Response Rates in Census Bureau Surveys," *Applied Marketing Research*, Vol. 30, No. 3, 1990, pp. 14-19.

2. Couper, Mick P. and Robert M. Groves (1993). "Household-Level Effects on Survey Participation," paper delivered at Fourth International Workshop on Household Survey Non-response, Bath, England, September 1993.

3. Courtland, Sherry, Chief, Demographic Surveys Division, Bureau of the Census, letter to Barbara Everitt Bryant, August 16, 1994.

4. *Ibid.*

5. Mesenbourg, Thomas, Assistant Director for Economic Programs, Bureau of the Census, letter to Barbara Everitt Bryant (undated), received August 19, 1994.

CHAPTER 11

How to Change the System

Americans may be wary and weary of the government asking them questions, but they're not shy about asking the government questions. Every day, telephone banks throughout the federal government field calls from people seeking statistical information.

Unfortunately, the experience can be frustrating. There are dozens of federal statistical agencies, and finding the right person at the right agency with the right number is difficult to say the least.

"People sometimes come here quite worn out," says Mark Mangold, a public information specialist at the Census Bureau. He tells the story of one caller who obviously had told her story many times.

"I listened. I sympathized," he said.

The caller, who first tried the public library, then the Environmental Protection Agency, and then the Department of Energy without success, was looking for statistics on the cost of pollution abatement.

"We could help," recalls Mangold, who, like other information specialists at the bureau, takes pride in providing answers quickly. While it's not widely known or even logical, the Census Bureau that counts people also gathers statistics on pollution abatement through the bureau's Industry Division.

"I knew what I was talking about. I think she called me a `treasure,'" recalls Mangold, chuckling at the flattery.

Information specialists at the Census Bureau and other

statistical agencies are invaluable when they rescue those lost in the data jungle, providing the elusive statistics they need or at least pointing them in the right direction.

Being bounced from agency to agency in search of a number feeds public cynicism and distrust toward the federal government. "My tax dollars at work," frustrated callers begin to mutter to themselves after the fourth or fifth phone call.

The difficulty in unearthing statistics also prevents people from realizing the full value of the information they supply to the government. A centralized source for statistical information would be the solution to this problem.

During March 1994, at a time when requests for data from the 1990 census had dropped off but questions about the economic censuses were high, the Census Bureau's customer services number (301-457-4100) fielded 7,300 calls for information. In another part of the Census Bureau, the Public Information Office (301-457-2794) logs 600 to 700 calls in a typical month, mostly from the media. Multiply these numbers several times over for all the other federal statistical agencies in Washington.

There is no central directory to guide people through the complex and confusing maze of the federal statistical system. That's why the Census Bureau's information specialists are so important and get so many frantic callers who beg them, "please, don't transfer me!"

If a camel is a horse designed by a committee, the federal statistical system is an animal whose design committee has yet to meet.

"If the federal statistical system were being built today," says former Census Bureau director Vince Barabba, "it would never wind up looking or functioning like it does now." He's not the first to say this, nor will he be the last. And while I agree with his opinion, unlike him I won't grace the collection of 10 major statistical agencies plus 60 other agencies that produce specialized statistics with the title "statistical system."

"A system," W. Edwards Deming told members of the American Statistical Association in 1993 in one of his last major public addresses, "is interdependent components that work together to try to accomplish an aim...A system must be managed."[1] There is little focused aim among the statistical agencies of the federal government, and the coordination of these agencies is only loosely managed.

Yet for reasons of history and protection of turf, more than for publicly expressed concerns about a centralized statistical agency, we do not seem able to fix the problem and create a true statistical system. Our neighbors to the north have nearly all of their federal statistics produced by one organization, Statistics Canada. In contrast, the Census Bureau is but one of many federal statistical agencies—though it is the largest. These agencies are scattered throughout different executive departments, with oversight and appropriations from different Congressional committees. Each statistical agency follows different laws regarding privacy and confidentiality, although all are covered by the Privacy Act of 1974.

Rather than forming a coherent system, the agencies are more like a group of noisy siblings who cooperate much of the time but also compete with one another for attention and resources. The consequences are not only duplication, waste, and confusion, but also public distrust, cynicism, and apathy.

Both the Census Bureau and the Internal Revenue Service measure income, produce population estimates, and calculate migration flows between states using some of the same data sources to do so. Both the Census Bureau and the Division of Vital Statistics at the National Center for Health Statistics collect data on marriage and divorce, one from surveys and censuses of those marrying and divorcing and the other from state records. Both the Census Bureau and the National Center for Education Statistics measure educational attainment.

Not all of what seems like duplication is wasteful. Much of it is deliberate. Collecting statistics in several different ways can provide a more accurate picture of the trends. The Bureau of Justice Statistics compiles and publishes data on the crimes people report to police, for example. In addition, the Justice Department contracts with the Census Bureau to survey a representative sample of households each year (the National Crime Victimization Survey), collecting data on the number of households victimized by crime—whether or not these crimes were reported to the police. The difference in the number of crimes reported to police versus the more comprehensive number of crimes reported by households reveals the percentage of crime that is not reported.

Fixing What's Broke

There is no doubt that the federal statistical system is in need of an overhaul.

About every ten years the idea of combining all federal statistical programs into a single agency is advanced. After review—and in the past even after extensive study—the idea is discarded, as it has been in recent years despite the intent to "reinvent government."

Janet Norwood has given such an overhaul a lot of thought. She is the undisputed "Dean Emerita" of statistical agency heads, having served three consecutive terms (1979 to 1991) as commissioner of the Bureau of Labor Statistics. According to Norwood, the federal statistical system evolved into its present framework when the world was far less complex and policy more narrow in scope. "As the government moved into new areas of activity and new cabinet departments were created, new specialized statistical organizations were formed within the new departments. These arrangements have for years served us well and, in fact, have provided statistical leadership to the world."

Pointing out how times and needs have changed, she says, "now we have a system of divided responsibility that limits our ability to act rapidly, develop comparability among data sets, develop state-of-the-art technology and take advantage of the economies and efficiencies of size." [2]

It's unlikely that any president will cash in his political chips to consolidate the many statistical agencies. Doing so would hurt his own political appointees by taking power away from the executive departments and cabinet members who head them. It's not likely that the Commerce Department would willingly hand over the Census Bureau or the Bureau of Economic Analysis to a central statistical agency. Nor would the Department of Labor want to give up the Bureau of Labor Statistics. The Department of Agriculture is not likely to give away its National Agricultural Statistics Service or Economic Research Service. Education will fight to keep the National Center for Education Statistics, just as Health and Human Services will fight for the National Center for Health Statistics and the Centers for Disease Control.

Most statistical agencies serve the specific missions of their departments. If the same statistics were to be produced by a central agency, each department would have to compete against all the others, standing in line to get what it wanted.

Proposals for combining statistical agencies go nowhere for another reason. Presidents would rather design programs that have more popular appeal. The production and coordination of statistics does not interest most people, though the use of those statistics is of vital importance to everyone.

"I don't know how you get excited about these numbers,"

Senator Warren Rudman of New Hampshire said to me in the Senate subcommittee hearing on adjustment. "They tend to put me to sleep." [3]

The federal government does provide some parental supervision of its statistical agency siblings. This supervision is performed by the Office of Statistical Policy within the Office of Management and Budget (OMB). The Office of Statistical Policy reviews and approves the budget requests of statistical agencies as a way of avoiding the duplication of activities. But in its supervisory role, the Office of Statistical Policy is more concerned with protecting Americans from paperwork—which invades the privacy of individuals, overburdens businesses, and takes the time of all—than with setting statistical priorities.

A primary mission of the Office of Statistical Policy is to approve the content and length of survey questionnaires. It does this not to coordinate statistical activities, but to reduce the amount of paperwork required of the public to fulfill the Paperwork Reduction Act. The office asks each agency to justify "respondent burden"—the number of minutes an individual or business will spend answering each survey multiplied by the number of respondents to be surveyed. This must be done for each survey or census conducted by the federal government, as well as those contracted out to academic and private-sector survey-research organizations.

The Office of Statistical Policy is understaffed. In recent years the office has had no more than ten professionals reviewing the substantive work of the government's statistical agencies. By comparison, the General Accounting Office has 40 people who review management and fiscal practices within those statistical agencies. In addition, the Office of Statistical Policy spends too much time trying to alleviate "respondent burden" rather than shaping the many federal statistical agencies into one true statistical system. Better coordination would do more to reduce the invasiveness of surveys and censuses, both in terms of privacy and time.

But the Office of Statistical Policy, although an overworked and frazzled parent, tries hard and is not short on ideas. In recent years it has attempted to arrange for the sharing of business establishment lists that are now maintained separately and differently by the Census Bureau and the Bureau of Labor Statistics. It developed draft legislation approved in concept by the Census Bureau, the Bureau of Economic Analysis, the Bureau of Labor Statistics, and the National Agricultural Statistics Service to create a data-sharing enclave among these four major agencies that would reduce duplicate activities and better protect respondent confidentiality. It encouraged the formation of a centralized data-information service, and it attempted to coordinate efforts of agencies throughout government to measure customer satisfaction. Most of these sound measures have yet to be implemented.

Norwood, now a senior fellow at the Urban Institute, is conducting a study of federal statistical agencies funded by the agencies themselves. According to Norwood, "The options probably lie somewhere between the increasing decentralization that we now have and the almost complete centralization that many other countries have."

Norwood suggests two possibilities: One, combining the larger organizations, such as the Commerce Department's Census Bureau and Bureau of Economic Analysis, the Labor Department's Bureau of Labor Statistics, and OMB's Office of Statistical Policy into one central statistical agency. At the same time, standardize in the other agencies the appointment of directors, their terms of office, and their degree of independence within departments. Two, abandon any attempt at centralization, but standardize operations and legislate confidentiality rules to protect survey respondents while allowing data to be shared within the system for statistical purposes. Norwood notes that at the same time, "we could strengthen coordination and leadership within the system and develop new approaches for review of statistical budgets both in the administration and in Congress."[4]

If the government standardized the way its statistical agencies work, it would mean making confidentiality requirements uniform from agency to agency. Today, the law varies depending on which statistical agency is taking a survey. The Census Bureau operates under Title 13, the most strict confidentiality requirement of all. There are no exceptions to Title 13. But other agencies follow different rules. Some have had confidentiality protection diluted by amendments to their laws, or confidentiality is so restricted that they cannot share data for statistical purposes or use it for analysis. For example, the National Center for Education Statistics (NCES) operates under confidentiality legislation that is similar to the Census Bureau's Title 13. By amendment, however, the data it gathers from certain longitudinal studies of individuals are exempt from this law, subject only to the comparatively lax provisions of the Privacy Act of 1974. Also by amendment, data collected by the NCES on individual schools are subject to the Privacy Act, though the Privacy Act was meant to apply only to individuals. This means any data the NCES collects through the National Assessment of Educational Progress cannot be used to determine the success of educational programs in different types of schools.

Here's another example of the convoluted operations of some of the federal statistical agencies: the Bureau of Labor Statistics does not have a statutory (by law) requirement to offer confidentiality to people who respond to its surveys. It has an informal policy of confidentiality, however—a policy that has been upheld by a district court. The Bureau of Labor Statistics obtains much of its data from state unemployment insurance agencies, which in turn follow a variety of laws protecting the confidentiality of their data. The Bureau of Labor Statistics cannot release these data without conforming to the states' laws.[5]

Ideally, standardized regulations regarding confidentiality would protect the identity of survey respondents but allow agencies to share data for statistical purposes.

I am not optimistic that "Statistics USA," my name for a centralized or semi-centralized agency comparable to Norwood's first alternative, is likely to happen given the politics of the situation—whether the administration is Democrat or Republican. There's no reason for a president to join this issue, and certainly there is no public pressure on individual members of Congress for statistical coordination. The idea of creating a single statistical agency has never gone far enough to become a public issue. If it were proposed, it might raise the unpopular vision of a Big Brother database. Consequently, the only likely scenario is greater standardization and coordination among existing agencies.

Other voices demanding better coordination are joining the choir. The Clinton Administration, under Vice President Gore's "reinventing government" initiative, formed a Statistics 2000 Task Force to identify ways to better coordinate economic statistics. The task force has identified what it calls "opportunities" for more data sharing among agencies. Some of these opportunities require legislation, which means change will happen slowly, if at all. Like other studies meant to streamline the federal government, such as the Grace Commission, this one offers some good ideas. But the federal government is slow to change, and with the public digging in its heels over the privacy issue, the changes may not happen at all.

However, with respect to economic statistics, the business media have taken up the single agency refrain. *Business Week*, for example, has noted more than once the need for better coordination:

> ...the dozens of statistical agencies throughout government have lost track of what is happening in the U.S. government. One agency would be better. [6]

> ...Congress and the government should take seriously statistics and their economic and financial impact. At the moment statistical agencies are largely orphaned. Paying attention means finally hiring a director of the Census Bureau and spending the dollars needed to get government statistics up to date...data collection is now divided among scores of offices and agencies throughout the government...This kind of bureaucratic feudalism is silly. At the very least agencies should be allowed to share company-level information—cooperation that is now illegal in many instances. [7]

And, after describing the overlap between agencies, *Business Week* writes:

> At a minimum this overlap should be eliminated. And it's time to go one step further. Canada has a single statistical agency, a model of effective data collection and analysis. [8]

Researchers are trying to resolve the conflicts between privacy and coordination. The National Academy of Sciences Panel on Confidentiality and Data Access has made recommendations on how to protect the confidentiality of respondents while at the same time promoting cooperation among statistical agencies. The panel recommended that, for all statistical agencies that do not have such regulations, the government should enact tough laws that protect the confidentiality of persons and organizations. This would bring other agencies up to the standards of the Census Bureau's Title 13 law.

The panel also recommended that the statistical records of all agencies be governed by a consistent set of rules and laws. There are too many inconsistencies and loopholes now. Additionally, the panel recommended that federal statistical agencies share individual data for statistical and research purposes, provided the confidentiality of records can be protected and with the proviso that the data not be used for regulatory or enforcement purposes.

Finally, the panel recommended more sharing of business lists for statistical purposes by federal and state agencies.[9]

This Is What We Must Do

Working in the federal statistical system tends to dampen idealism. While I favor a centralized statistical system, I'm cynical enough now to know that Statistics USA is not likely to happen. But something must be done to protect our economic well-being in a fast-moving global economy. Americans must be persuaded to put aside their fears to salvage their collective knowledge of themselves.

If we can't have a Statistics USA, then five changes to our current system are desirable and feasible. Having headed the largest statistical agency—and hindsight providing 20/20 vision—I recommend:

1. "One-Stop Shopping" Information Service. The credit for this idea goes to Katherine Wallman, chief of the Office of Statistical Policy at OMB. You can't tell the players without a program, whether you're at a baseball game or in need of federal statistics. If Americans had easy access to federal statistics, already published and protected by strict laws of confidentiality, their use of government statistics would increase and their fear of the misuse of statistics might be alleviated. At least the benefits of the government's data collection efforts would be more obvious. So far, Wallman has not been able to implement a one-stop-shopping service because there is no budget for centralizing statistical activities.

It's time for a national hotline. Call it something like 1-900-DATANOW, a computerized information service that is updated hourly. Call this number and it will tell you what numbers are available and guide you to the right agency to get them. Knowledge is power. Why not put our tax dollars to work empowering Americans?

2. An Enclave for Sharing Data Among Statistical Agencies. The government's statistical agencies could eliminate a lot of duplication if they were allowed to share the data they now collect. Both the Census Bureau and the Bureau of Labor Statistics build and maintain separate lists of every business establishment in the country, for example. Each agency uses its list to select businesses to include in sample surveys.

The Census Bureau's list is continually updated with information collected from its economic censuses and surveys. The Bureau of Labor Statistics updates its list with data provided by individual states from payroll and unemployment compensation filings. Each agency has promised confidentiality to the businesses and states that provide data. Thus, each is prevented from sharing its list with the other.

These lists should be combined and serve both agencies, saving money and time. To do so requires legislation. We need to create a data enclave that would permit data sharing among agencies. This enclave would not include regulatory agencies, however, because people would refuse to talk to statistical agencies if they knew the information would be made available to enforcement officials. Many people would refuse to report their income in censuses and surveys if they knew the Census Bureau gave the information to the IRS for tax enforcement. And, as mentioned earlier, a business would be unlikely to reveal what it spends on pollution abatement if that information were given to the Environmental Protection Agency, which enforces anti-pollution regulations.

3. Standardize Appointment and Reporting. Currently, the heads of statistical agencies come in a variety of forms. Some are presidential appointees with fixed terms, such as the commissioner of the Bureau of Labor Statistics and the director of the National Center for Education Statistics. Others are presidential appointees who must leave office with the president who named them, such as the director of the Bureau of the Census and the director of the Bureau of Justice Statistics. Still others are career civil servants, such as those who head both statistical agencies in the Department of Agriculture and the Bureau of Economic Analysis.

Some of the statistical agency heads report directly to the secretaries of their respective departments. The commissioner of the Bureau of Labor Statistics reports directly to the secretary of labor, for example. It's a different story in the Department of Commerce, where the director of the Census Bureau reports to the under secretary for economic affairs. The under secretary, in turn, reports to the secretary of commerce. But 95 percent of the budget and employees of the under secretary are in the Census Bureau, adding an extra level of bureaucracy that must be worked through with each of the bureau's budget requests, major personnel appointments, and even for approval of every public information news release. Whenever there is a 95 percent overlap in the roles of two administrators—as there is with the Census Bureau's director and the under secretary for economic affairs—the result is inevitable conflict, whatever their personalities. The director of the Census Bureau should report directly to the secretary of commerce.

The appointments of the heads of all statistical agencies should be standardized. The current differences are one factor fracturing the system. All agency heads should have fixed-term appointments, giving them the power that comes with presidential appointment and also the independence and objectivity that they need to do the job right. A fixed term means they cannot be fired if they make a politically unpopular decision. The statistical system is best served by those who put accuracy above expediency.

While four-year terms may be logical for most agency heads, it is not logical for the director of the Census Bureau. Because of the unique cycle of the population census, the director of the Census Bureau should have a five-year term beginning in years ending in one and six. This would prevent a repeat of the situation in which I found myself in 1989 and which George Hay Brown (who advocates a ten-year term) found himself in 1969, parachuting into the Census Bureau just months before the enormous census operation.

4. Centralize Appropriations for Statistical Agencies. Nothing would help coordinate statistical activities more than the centralization of appropriations in Congress. Consider the case of the Current Population Survey (CPS), the nation's largest ongoing monthly survey of the population. Since 1942, the CPS has been conducted by the Census Bureau for the Bureau of Labor Statistics.

In the late 1980s and early 1990s, the CPS needed to be redesigned to reflect the changing labor force. But creating a new questionnaire, introducing computer-assisted-interviewing, and redesigning the sample to use population and household data from the 1990 census required budgetary approval for both the BLS and the Census Bureau. Yet in the Congressional appropriations process, there is no way to coordinate the budget requests of the two agencies since one is in the Department of Labor and the other in the Department of Commerce. At one critical juncture, Congress funded the request of the BLS but cut the Census Bureau's request, though both agencies were jointly modernizing the survey.

This is only one example among many. The problem is that the funding for each of the federal government's statistical agencies is determined by whatever subcommittee is charged with appropriations for that department. A statistical system needs unified budgeting.

5. Empower the Office of Statistical Policy. If we don't have a centralized statistical system, then we need more resources spent on coordination of what we have. The Office of Statistical Policy in the Office of Management and Budget is understaffed and underfunded. It needs a boost.

If I were still the director of the Census Bureau, I would not enjoy more direction from OMB, but I should have to accept it. The chief of the Office of Statistical Policy should have some of the decision-making clout and ability to speak for the system that the chief statisticians have in Canada and Australia. A statistical system needs someone with the power to set priorities, broker appropriations requests, distribute resources, and eliminate duplication. With more resources and a better-defined mission, the Office of Statistical Policy could do this.

As Norwood says, and her 20/20 hindsight vision is honed by more years of experience at the top of a statistical agency than mine: "We've got a system that is becoming increasingly fragmented. That's all right except that...we have to pay the price for coordinating it. If that weakness of management is not corrected, it will lead to disaster." [10]

References

1. Deming, W. Edwards, "Theory of a System," address to the Joint Statistical Meeting, San Francisco, California, August 9, 1993 (from notes taken by Barbara Everitt Bryant).

2. Norwood, Janet (1993). "Statistics: A New Beginning," *Chance*, Vol. 6, No. 1, 1993, p. 44.

3. "Quote of the Week," *New York Newsday*, July 22, 1991, p. 14.

4. Norwood, p. 44.

5. Panel on Confidentiality and Data Access, Committee on National Statistics, Commission on Behavioral and Social Sciences and Education, National Research Council, Social Sciences Research Council (1993), *Private Lives and Public Policies*, (Washington DC: National Academy Press, 1993), pp. 109-140.

6. "Where to Prune and Where to Hack," *Business Week*, September 13, 1993, p. 98.

7. "Bad Policy Starts With Bad Numbers," *Business Week*, July 18, 1994, p. 102.

8. Gleckman, Howard (1994). "Uncle Sam's Stats: Call Them Unreliable," *Business Week*, July 18, 1994, p. 40.

9. Panel on Confidentiality and Data Access, pp. 219-227.

10. Interview with Janet Norwood, "Good Policy Builds on Reliable Data," *Challenge*, July-August 1993, p. 18.

CHAPTER 12

The 21st Century Census

It is mid-March in the year 2000. Your postal carrier has just delivered a letter to your home. The letter might be from the president of the United States—for maximum impact. More likely it will come from a successor of mine at the Census Bureau. The letter tells you to expect the 2000 census questionnaire next week in your mail.

When the questionnaire arrives, you set it aside—as so many people do. Two days later you get a reminder in the mail, asking you to fill out the questionnaire.

If you didn't get a questionnaire, there are other ways you can answer the census. In a few places, you can answer the census interactively by computer, touching a screen to respond to questions. After you've answered one question, another pops up: "What is your age?" It takes only about three minutes to answer all the questions. If you're wondering how this information is used, you can ask the computer to tell you. A video presentation appears on the screen, probably someone from your own community, explaining the local benefits of the census.

The Census Bureau tested this type of interactive kiosk in the 1995 test census in Paterson, New Jersey. The technology works, but the kiosks cost too much to use extensively in 2000.

By 2010, however, such kiosks will be everywhere. You'll probably use them to buy stamps in the local post office, to buy tickets at train and airport terminals, and to retrieve reference material at your library. The Census Bureau will probably rent time on these kiosks to allow people to answer the 23rd census of the United States.

In 2000, however, the most likely alternative to filling out a questionnaire at home will be dialing an 800-number and answering the census by phone. You will have this option offered to you if you haven't returned your mailed questionnaire within a few weeks, or if you speak a language other than English or Spanish. When you call the 800-number, you might not talk to a human being. By 2000, computers that recognize a wide range of voices and dialects will be able to question you and enter your answers directly into the census database.

If for any reason the computer can't understand you or you can't understand it, it will be programmed to call for help. It will switch you over to a computer-assisted-telephone-interviewing (CATI) terminal operated by a real, live person.

The Census Bureau did not use CATI technology in 1990, although this technology was well developed. In 2000, the bureau will use CATI in a big way to save time and money and to offer a customer-friendly way to answer the census, or to call those who have not responded.

The 2000 census questionnaire will be easier to read and fill out than the questionnaires of 1970, 1980, or 1990. Questionnaires will be available in a variety of places for those who misplace theirs—or for those whose addresses haven't made it into the greatly improved master address file. You will be able to pick one up at city hall, the unemployment office, the post office, or at the local shopping mall.

In previous censuses, the Census Bureau has been stingy with questionnaires, fearing that special interest groups might try to stuff the ballot box to boost their population count. By 2000 there will be a number of computerized ways to check for duplication efficiently, allowing the Census Bureau to distribute questionnaires freely.

If your address is on the master address file and you haven't returned your questionnaire or phoned in within four weeks, you'll receive one final mailing. This one will include another questionnaire, bar-coded with the location of your housing unit, as was the original. The enclosed letter will ask you again to fill out and return the questionnaire or call one of the 800 numbers. You will also be informed that answering the census is the law.

The master address file will be much better than it was in 1990. It will have been continually updated by the U.S. Postal Service for one thing, and the Census Bureau will work more closely with cities and local communities to ensure accuracy.

With the law restricting access to the address list relaxed to allow sharing with local governments, the Census Bureau will be able to show cities its address lists (containing no names) and let the cities compare them with their own. A list of actual addresses will be much easier to compare with tax rolls and other records than the block numbers and housing unit counts the bureau gave cities in 1990. It is hoped that the Census Bureau and the cities can thus work cooperatively rather than confronting each other in courtrooms later.

In 2000, as in 1990, local communities will be asked to help promote the count to their constituencies. Census awareness specialists will target local groups for promotion. But no matter how hard the bureau tries to cooperate with the cities, some mayors will insist that their populations are greater than the number counted by the census.

Count on the Undercount

And they will be right. Despite improvements in census taking, the undercount probably will be even larger in 2000 than it was in 1990. Americans are becoming harder to count as they become more diverse. And we are becoming much more diverse.

Hard-to-enumerate segments of the population are growing much faster than the population as a whole, including those in non-family households, those not living in any household, and Blacks, Hispanics, and Asians. In 2000 there will be many more immigrants in the population than there were in 1990 because of new immigration laws that took effect in 1991 to increase legal visas. And there is little evidence that we have managed to stem illegal immigration. The Mexican border is too long; the straits of Florida too narrow; tourist visas too easy to get and overstay. Immigrants are less likely to answer the census because many fear government. They do not believe that one branch of government, the Census Bureau, does not talk to another branch, like the immigration service or the local police, because this may not have been true where they came from.

There is only so much the Census Bureau can do to count everyone. The bureau doesn't have—nor does it want—search warrants to determine how many people really live in each housing unit. The Constitution requires a census, but it also protects people from unlawful searches.

The One-Number Census

If the trends of the past few decades continue, those in 35 to 45 percent of housing units won't return the 2000 census form. Perhaps 10 percent of these units will turn out to be vacant, including seasonal homes. But that leaves a considerable 25 to 35 percent of households who, either from intent or apathy, fail to cooperate with the census effort.

Then there are others who won't get counted for one reason or another: perhaps they are homeless; perhaps they live in a housing unit that did not make it onto the master address file—there are bound to be some, although we hope it will be fewer than in 1990; or perhaps they were not included on the census form filled out and returned by others living in the housing unit. What do we do about this problem? How do we protect people's privacy but still collect the information we so desperately need to function efficiently as a democracy and as a market economy? How can we minimize the undercount and still rein in the cost of census taking?

The answer lies in using statistical techniques. First, we must do an intensive follow-up, but only on a sample of nonrespondents rather than everyone. The Census Bureau spends months trying to interview those who do not want to cooperate with the census. As the months drag on, the efforts to count the missing became more prone to error.[1] Interviewers ring door bells and climb to fifth-floor apartments time and again. In the end, they often have to resort to asking neighbors about the characteristics of the people they can't find.

It's time to start using more brains and less brawn—and a lot less money. It's an enormous effort to track down 30 million to 40 million reluctant households. It cost between $490 million and $560 million in 1990.[2] It can only be done imperfectly. The Census Bureau could do a more accurate job of counting Americans and collecting information about their characteristics if it followed-up on perhaps only one-third of the missing households. The bureau could use that information to estimate the characteristics of the rest of the missing.

Second, we should conduct a second census of a sample of blocks that have already been counted and that interviewers have already followed-up to determine how many people are still missing. In 1990 this was the post-enumeration survey, the results of which were not available until 1991. That produced the two-number census—an enumerated count and an adjusted count. The two numbers set in motion intense political pressures, with some politicians changing sides depending on which number produced the largest count for his or her constituency. Next time around, the second census of a sample of blocks needs to be done during the census process, with the findings used to correct the count delivered to the president by December 31.

The one-number census is produced by combining the results of the census forms returned voluntarily, plus the estimate from the non-response follow-up, plus the estimate of the undercounted from the second census of a sample of blocks, then subtracting the estimate of the overcounted.

What About Those Who Won't Cooperate?

What do we do about those who won't cooperate with the follow-up or second census of a sample of blocks? How do we honor their rights to privacy and still collect the information our society needs? Should the Census Bureau gain access to other government records so that it can match the addresses of those who refuse to cooperate with the addresses of program recipients, taxpayers, voters, or students? Where is the line between privacy rights and the public good?

The Census Bureau should have access to those records—but only as a last resort and if it uses the information only for statistical purposes—to ascertain the number and characteristics of people who live in an area. As with those who answer the census, the names of those counted through other government records would not be linked to their characteristics until the National Archives opens individual census records 72 years later.

Even the one-number census will not be 100 percent accurate. What's more, no one will ever know what 100 percent accuracy is. No one can guarantee to the mayor of New York City, or Oakland, California, or—yes, Salina, Kansas—that the census is perfect. What can be guaranteed is that the number is as

Design for a one-number census

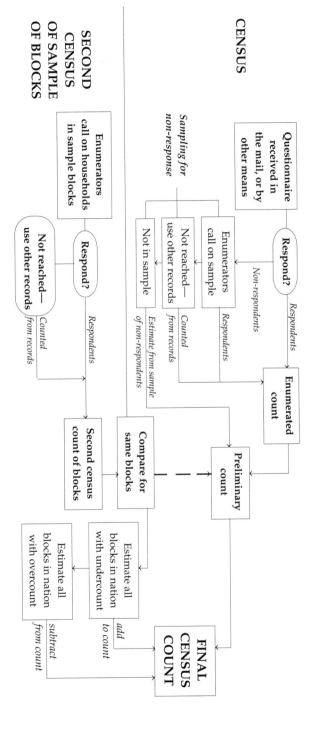

accurate as possible because it is based on state-of-the-art enumeration and statistical techniques. Will the American people accept that? Will their mayors? I hope so.

Getting an Outside Perspective

My ideas for 2000 have evolved from my role in overseeing the 1990 census, evaluating what worked and what did not work. These ideas were taking shape in my thinking when I left the Census Bureau at the end of January 1993. They have been refined by the results of Census Bureau research, which I have followed closely even after leaving the bureau. They are views I developed independently of studies by two National Academy of Sciences/National Research Council panels. I had some role in establishing one of those panels—the Panel to Evaluate Alternative Census Methods. When we decided to research fundamental change in census taking, we also decided not to go it alone at the Census Bureau. We wanted objective outside evaluation, and thus we funded the Panel to Evaluate Alternative Census Methods. Our critics also wanted independent evaluation of the direction the census should take. Thus our Congressional appropriations subcommittee required that we use some of our budget to fund the Panel on Census Requirements in the Year 2000 and Beyond. Both panels published interim reports in 1993. [3,4]

By the end of 1994, the Panel to Evaluate Alternative Census Methods had published its final report and recommendations. [5] Happily, I am in agreement with most of its recommendations, probably because many match my own. There are other recommendations in its report, *Counting People in the Information Age*, which I support but realistically don't think can come to pass. The panel doesn't have to deal with the Commerce Department's competing needs, its budgeting process, or the Congressional subcommittee on appropriations. I did.

In November 1994, the second National Academy of Sciences/National Research Council Panel checked in, agreeing with the position I advocate here: The Census Bureau must use statistical sampling techniques to supplement its actual head count in 2000. [6,7]

For 2000, the Census Bureau must strike a balance between what would be ideal, what is cost-effective, and what can get funded. The 1990 census was adequately funded, but many operations were not efficient. The research since then, coupled with the recommendations of the National Research Council as well as the ideas presented in this book should pay off in making the 2000 census more cost-effective and accurate. But this can happen only if the Census Bureau is unfettered by lawsuits and by the controversies engendered by those whose agenda is greed—getting the most money and power—rather than the most accurate count possible.

Protecting Our Privacy

Americans probably have more privacy than the citizens of any other country in the world. Unlike many countries, we have no population register. The federal government has our census records, our Social Security records, and our tax returns. Someday the government may have our health records as well. These are records that include most of us, but none include all of us. Each record may contain some facts about us, but no record contains all the facts about us.

Rightfully, Americans have more to fear about the invasion of their privacy today than they did before there were computerized databases. But our privacy is being invaded not by the government, but by businesses that buy and sell mailing lists. We voluntarily join those lists each time we apply for a loan, subscribe to a magazine, order from a catalog, or send in a warranty card for an appliance. As Chris Hibbert of Computer Professionals for Social Responsibility told members of the American Statistical Association, "Protecting privacy in the computer age is like trying to change a tire on a fast-moving vehicle."[8]

When I bought an electric coffee maker recently, it came with an offer to add my name to a $250 sweepstakes "to thank me for taking the time to fill out this short questionnaire." The questionnaire asked for my address, which appliances I owned, whether I bought the coffee maker as a gift, which factors influenced my purchase decision, and what credit cards I use. It also asked whether I was a veteran, whether I buy items through the mail regularly, have a dog or cat, support health charities, belong to a frequent flyer program, and which of 50 sports and leisure activities I participate in regularly.

If I had succumbed to the lure of thinking I might win $250, this "short questionnaire" would have expanded the direct mail I receive exponentially. The company that wanted this information cannot get my name or address from the census, but through my address it can link my responses on its questionnaire to census data about my neighborhood (of 300 to 400 households, the smallest level of geography for which census data are released).

Some may feel incensed about this use of information. Yet we would not be the nation we are without it. We would not be able to buy a specialty coffee maker, choose from 100,000 items at a local discount store, or shop at a supermarket with 50 different types of cereal if we did not know what we know about one another. Our market economy has been able to provide us with the standard of living we now enjoy because we have statistics on who we are, what we do, what we want, and how we are changing.

The free market of goods and services and the free market

of ideas are built—at least in part—on a base of facts and figures. The burning issues of the day—health-care reform, educational standards, crime prevention, environmental protection, the information highway, are all driven by statistics. At the heart of these statistics stands the Census Bureau.

More Data for the 21st Century

Instead of hiding our heads in the sand, it's time to demand more. Taking a snapshot of the nation every ten years is not enough. California gained 6 million people during the 1980s, and three out of four were immigrants. Anyone trying to plan schools, hospitals, bus routes, or anything else in Los Angeles at the end of the 1980s was flying blind—until 1990 census data became available in 1991.

We fly blind during part of every decade, once census results are out of date. While the Census Bureau produces annual estimates of the populations of states, and biennial estimates of the populations of cities and counties, while private companies sell estimates of populations at the local level, and while the Current Population Survey tracks changes in demographic characteristics at the national level, these statistics show only the broad outlines. They don't show the important details about what's happening in Los Angeles, or Cleveland, or Steelville, Missouri—the location of the center of population in 1990.

What might have been adequate during the 19th century was barely adequate for the last half of the 20th century and will not be enough for the 21st. It is time to rethink our data-collection efforts.

We need the one-number census to get an accurate population count for the nation and small areas every ten years. But we need to simplify what's collected on the census, combining it with large ongoing surveys throughout the decade that provide continuously updated profiles of the population and details of our demographic, economic, and geographic characteristics. While we will save some money by shortening the census questionnaire and following-up on only a sample of non-respondents, these savings will not be enough to pay for large through-the-decade surveys of the population. But we should not consider direct cost alone. We must consider the economic benefits of up-to-date data every year for the states, and every several years (by combining surveys) for thousands of communities across the country. It would be money well spent.

Welcome to Democracy

March 3, 1994: The headline in *The New York Times* reads: "When Russia's Census-Takers Call, A Bitter Reception Can Await Them."[9]

The headline grabbed my attention because, a few years earlier, I had met with Vadim N. Kirichenko when he visited the Census Bureau. At the time, Kirichenko was the director of Goskomstat, the State Committee on Statistics of the former USSR. He described census-taking in the USSR. Compared to the U.S., it sounded easy. Every citizen already had his or her name on a government list. Every citizen obediently answered any questions asked by local government census takers. The government then simply tallied the responses. With no system for litigation, Moscow couldn't sue Goskomstat!

Now, four years later, things had changed.

"The questions posed by census takers are drawing some angry answers from Russians discontented with their lot and reluctant to cooperate," reported *The New York Times* article. It described the efforts of one census taker who was interviewing a Svetlana A. Berikova and her family, asking how the Berikova family was making out in the new Russia.

I felt like shouting across the thousands of miles to Mrs. Berikova: "Answer your census! You can't build a free market economy without good facts and figures."

And to the 19-year-old census taker, I wanted to say: "Keep at it—and welcome to democracy!"

References

1. Erickson, Eugene P. and Teresa K. DeFonso (1993). "Beyond the Net Undercount: How to Measure Census Error," *Chance*, Vol. 6, No. 4, Spring 1993, pp. 38-43.

2. Panel to Evaluate Alternative Census Methods, Committee on National Statistics, Commission on Behavioral and Social Sciences and Education, National Research Council (1994), *Counting People in the Information Age*, (Washington, D.C.: National Academy Press, 1994), p. 98.

3. Panel to Evaluate Alternative Census Methods, Committee on National Statistics, Commission on Behavioral and Social Sciences and Education, National Research Council (1993), *A Census That Mirrors America: Interim Report*, (Washington, D.C.: National Academy Press, 1993).

4. Panel on Census Requirements in the Year 2000 and Beyond, Committee on National Statistics, Commission on Behavioral and Social Sciences and Education, National Research Council (1993), *Planning the Decennial Census: Interim Report*, Panel on Census Requirements in the Year 2000 and Beyond, Committee on National Statistics, (Washington, D.C.: National Academy Press, 1993).

5. Panel to Evaluate Alternative Census Methods (1994).

6. Holmes, Steven A. (1994). "Census is Urged to Use Statistical Sampling," *The New York Times*, November 18, 1994, p. A10.

7. Panel on Census Requirements in the Year 2000 and Beyond, Committee on National Statistics, Commission on Behavioral and Social Sciences and Education, National Research Council (1995). *Modernizing the U.S. Census*, (Washington, D.C.: National Academy Press, 1995).

8. Hibbert, Chris, presentation to a session of the Joint Statistical Meeting, Toronto, August 16, 1994.

9. Speder, Michael (1994). "When Russia's Census-Takers Call, A Bitter Reception Can Await Them," *The New York Times*, March 3, 1994, p. A6.

Postscript

Did I have fun? I have been asked this question countless times by friends, as well as the occasional stranger, upon learning who I was in my previous life.

My answer is unequivocal and always the same: "Yes! Absolutely!"

But, did I have a normal life? With adjustment decisions, a commuter marriage, and an in-box that filled up each day like a recycling bin, the answer has to be "no."

My husband John, an electronic engineer whose contribution to the 1990 census was tolerating a long-distance relationship for four years, is glad to have me back in town. I'm glad to be living a more normal life with him.

Still, as I said when I left the bureau: "I have been to the mountain top. The Census Bureau is the dream of survey researchers: sample sizes are big, resources are substantial, the subject matter is fascinating, and the data are hot. So hot that they end up in court. Like other mountain tops, this one was both rocky and exhilarating."[1]

Would I have liked to stay longer? Yes, I would have liked another term to follow through on three activities that began while I was the director. One, research on fundamental change for census 2000—such as sampling non-respondents to reduce cost, building estimation into the census-taking process to account for those missed, and combining a simpler decennial census with large ongoing surveys to produce up-to-date information about Americans. Two, to continue the implementation of quality management processes in the Census Bureau. Three, to see the full implementation of computer-assisted survey information collection.

Happily, these three projects are moving forward since my departure. And I knew when I took the presidential appointment that the job was not for someone who needed job security.

What I Don't Miss

What I don't miss is working through six layers of federal bureaucracy. That's what the Census Bureau faces just to get its budget approved, a process that lasts over a year. First the budget must be reviewed by the under secretary for economic affairs. Then it is reviewed by the secretary of commerce and balanced with competing requests within the department, becoming a part of the Commerce Department's proposed budget. Third, the Office of Management and Budget reviews it, usually requesting supporting documentation and defense by the bureau's director. After final OMB review, the request becomes part of the president's budget. Fourth, the Subcommittee for Commerce, Justice, State, and the Judiciary of the House Appropriations Committee reviews the bureau's budget, again requiring defense by the director. It then moves on to the full committee and finally to House vote. Fifth, the proposed budget is then reviewed by the Senate. Sixth and finally, the House-Senate Conference Committee must agree on the budget.

At each level of bureaucracy, the budget gets cut. Six potential cuts in the budget means the bureau cannot enter the budget process with a realistic funding proposal.

Meanwhile back at headquarters in Suitland, the bureau staff is operating under the current budget, developing a budget request for two years hence, and defending next year's budget. Is it any wonder I don't miss the process?

I'm also glad to be back in a world where I can write letters that don't have to be reviewed by lawyers fearful of their impact on the outcome of census adjustment lawsuits or checked for conformance with Census Bureau and Commerce Department policies.

A letter I wrote in response to one I received from Senator Paul S. Sarbanes on July 27, 1992, was finally hand-delivered to him more than six weeks later, on September 8. It took that long to reply because the letter had to go through about 16 steps, at least 2 of which included my refusal to sign obtuse versions that did not answer Sarbanes' questions. By the time he got my response, I'm sure he thought we were trying to hide something, which we weren't. Today I can sit at my word processor, type "Dear Senator Sarbanes," and pop the letter in the mail. But Sarbanes no longer writes to ask me any questions!

I also don't miss the organization chart of the Census Bureau, which in my term I managed to change but never to flatten. It's not much different from the way other federal departments and agencies are organized—which is to say there are far too many layers. The entire organizational structure of the federal government needs to become much more horizontal to function efficiently in the 21st century.

What I Do Miss

Hard as it might be to believe, I sometimes miss Congressional hearings, sparring with the likes of Rep. Charles Schumer or answering tough questions from senators and representatives on the census oversight subcommittees, or from reporters on the census beat. I deeply miss my role in producing data that describe real Americans and how our dynamic economy is evolving. I also miss the people with whom I worked in the Census Bureau, the Department of Commerce, at OMB, and in the other statistical agencies.

As Ben Wattenberg wrote in *This USA*, his book about the 1960 census, "...the census is such a valuable document largely because of the dedicated men and women who work at the Bureau of the Census. I am not an authority on Washington, or on government, or on what is called 'bureaucracy,' but if bureaucracy is typified by the operations to be found in the census building—I'd buy more of it immediately. There was pride, quality, thought and efficiency in such census labors as I witnessed..."[2]

The successors to the people who worked at the Census Bureau in 1960 are just as dedicated and competent today. The value of their data is just as great, and the data are more accessible to the public than they were 30 years ago.

Today I'm happily in the midst of the design and administration of the American Customer Satisfaction Index, a new economic indicator of quality launched in 1994 by the School of Business Administration at the University of Michigan and the American Society for Quality Control. I'm also involved in management consulting through Anjoy QSP, an international private-sector firm. But if whoever is president in 1999 finds a need for someone who can parachute into the 2000 census—well, I'm experienced and can be found in Ann Arbor, Michigan.

References

1. Bryant, Barbara Everitt (1993). "Reflections of the Census Director," *American Demographics*, March 1993, pp. 13-15.

2. Wattenberg, Ben J. (1965). *This USA: An Unexpected Family Portrait of 194,067,296 Americans Drawn From the Census*, in collaboration with Richard M. Scammon (Garden City, New Jersey: Doubleday, 1965), p. 312.

Index

Baltimore, MD, 106, 136
Bar-code scanners/bar-coded, 80, 85, 207
Barabba, Vincent, 43-45, 51, 140-141, 190
Barringer, Felicity, 119, 143
Beijing, 78
Beltaire, Beverly, 53
Berikova, Svetlana, 216-217
Berra, Yogi, 42
Betts, Jackson, 59
Beverly, Lynn, 129
Bienville Parish, LA, 12
Billings, John, 80-81
Binghamton, NY, 85
Blacks, undercount, 2, 151, 164
Block group, 25, 34
Boehme, Frederick G., 29-33
Boston, MA, 131, 135
Boston Common, Boston, MA, 135
Bounpane, Peter, 100, 149
Brinkley, David, 131
Broome, Harmon, 129
Brown, George Hay, 202
Brown, Ronald, 118-119, 160
Brown, Willie, 52-53
Bryant, Jake, 174
Bryant, John H., 49, 219
Bryant, Linda (Linda Bryant Valentine), 49
Bryant, Lois (Lois Bryant Chen), 49, 117
Bryant, Randal E., 49
Budget, Census Bureau, 15, 220
Bureau of Economic Analysis, 62, 193, 195, 201
Bureau of Justice Statistics. *See* Justice, Department of
Bureau of Labor Statistics, 168, 171, 177-178, 192-193, 195-197, 200-203
Bush administration, 21, 38, 158, 175

Bush, President George H. W. 1, 55, 109, 133, 142-143, 158
Business Week, 198

C-Span, 101, 112, 115, 122
California, 46, 51-52, 129, 131-132, 137, 166, 179, 210, 215
Canada, 191, 198, 203
Cannon House Office Building, 108, 115
Capitol Hill/The Hill, 5, 91, 108, 117
Carey vs. Klutznick, 140-141
Carling, Jan, 76
Carnegie Commission on Science, Technology, and Government, 47
Carson City, CA, 95
Carter, President Jimmy, 42, 48, 142
CASIC (Computer Assisted Survey Information Collection), 84-85, 220
Castor Spanish GS&B, 96
CATI. *See* Computer-assisted-telephone-interviewing
CBS, 115, 143
CD-ROMs/CDs/Compact Disks, 71, 83, 85, 185
Census
    block group, 25, 34
    cost, 2, 7-8, 17, 120, 209
    data uses, 61-65
    employment, 87, 128
    history, 6
    lawsuits, 2, 19, 140-141, 158
    mailing/return, 15-17, 114, 124-133, 181
    questionnaire, 8-9, 15-17, 60-61
    tract, 25, 34
Census/1790, 6, 60, 83
Census/1790-1910, 30, 80-81
Census/1920, 30-31, 35, 161
Census/1930, 31
Census/1940, 150-151

225

Nixon, President Richard, 43
Non-blacks, undercount, 151, 164
North Carolina, 68, 71
   12th District, 68, 71-72
Northeast, 44, 148, 161, 166
Northwestern University, 152
Norwood, Janet, 192-193, 195-197, 203

Oakland, CA, 9-10, 12
Office of Management and Budget
   (OMB), 178, 220-221
Office of Statistical Policy, 194-195,
   199, 203
Ogilvy and Mather, 96
Ohio, 166
Oklahoma, 160
Old Farmer's Almanac, 185-186
Ongoing surveys plus census, 9, 215-
   216, 219
One man (person), one vote, 67
One-number census, 168, 208-211
One-stop shopping information ser-
   vice, 199
Outreach campaign, 1990 census, 92-
   98
Owner-occupied housing, residents of,
   undercount, 2, 164

P/R Associates, 53
Pacific Islanders, 95
Palm Springs, CA, 131
Panama, 115
Panel on Census Requirements for the
   Year 2000 and Beyond, 212-213
Panel on Confidentiality and Data
   Access, 26, 198
Panel to Evaluate Alternative Census
   Methods, 212
Pantograph punch, 81
Paperwork Reduction Act, 194
Paterson, NJ, 9, 14, 205

Pemberton, David M., 29-33
Pennsylvania, 160, 166
Pennsylvania State University, 152
Plant, Mark, 110, 154
Plotkin, Emmanuel, 42
Plum Book, 46-47
Population estimates, 162-171
   director decision not to adjust, 167
Population registers/registry, 22-23,
   76
Port Authority Bus Terminal, New
   York, NY, 91, 101, 103
Porter, Robert, 81
Post-enumeration survey, 1, 152-171,
   209
Presidential appointment/appointee,
   1, 56, 201-202, 220
Privacy Act of 1974, 36-38, 121, 191-
   196
Privacy Protection Commission, 27
Privacy, 2, 6-41, 120-122, 125-126, 180,
   191, 197, 209-210, 213-215. *See also*
   Confidentiality
Prune Book, 47
Puerto Rico, 86-87, 97-98
Punch cards, 81

Quality management, 220
Queen Elizabeth II of Great Britain,
   94-95
Questionnaire, census, 8-9, 15-17, 60-
   61
   questions, 60-61

Reagan, President Ronald, 46, 48
Reapportionment, 3, 30-31, 44, 67, 109,
   111, 143, 160
Recess appointment, 55-56, 109
Red River Parish, LA, 12
Redistricting, 3, 44, 67-72, 111
Remington-Rand, 82

New Strategist

Reference Books for Market Researchers
from New Strategist Publications

The Official Guide to the American Marketplace

Clearly written and critically acclaimed, *The Official Guide to the American Marketplace* is the ultimate guide to trends in race and ethnicity, income, spending, health, education, living arrangements, population, and much more. *"The Official Guide to the American Marketplace* should be on your bookshelf." —*The Wall Street Journal*

The Official Guide to American Incomes

The demographics of buying power—who's making more, who's making less, and how much they have left over after buying the basics. This comprehensive look at how much Americans have to spend was one of *Library Journal*'s Best Reference Sources of 1993.

The Official Guide to Household Spending

The #1 guide to how much consumers spend on everything from entertainment to food, housing to personal care, apparel to gifts—over 1,000 products and services in all, broken out by 26 demographic characteristics. "...an invaluable resource for our sales and marketing efforts," —Susan Smollens, V.P., Rsch. & Mktg. Svcs., Hachette Magazines, Inc.

The Official Guide to the Generations

Age and generational identity are crucial factors in understanding consumer behavior. This insightful new book analyzes the demographics, incomes, and spending patterns of today's age groups and shows marketers how to benefit from their similarities and differences.

Coming in 1996

The Official Guides to Regional Markets:
Northeast, Midwest, South, West

Four volumes examining the demographics, incomes, and spending patterns of the nation' regions, states, and metropolitan areas of 1 million or more.

New Strategist Publications, Inc.

Post Office Box 242 • Ithaca, New York 14851 • 607/273-0913